Sustainable Organizations

The Role of Smart Technologies

Winston W. H. Weng

Decision Analysis for
Sustainable Development
From the Aspects of
Technology and Strategy

Sustainable Organizations:

The Role of Smart Technologies

Winston W. H. Weng

Decision Analysis for
Sustainable Development
From the Aspects of
Technology and Strategy

Sustainable Organizations: The Role of Smart Technologies

Contents

Preface ... Preface-1

About the author ... Author-1

Chapter 1 ... 1-1

Emerging information technologies and Competitive Strategies

Chapter 2 ... 2-1

Internet of Things and Marketing Intelligence

Chapter 3 ... 3-1

Big Data Analytics and Supply Chain Competence

Preface

This book elucidates the interrelationships among the three core elements of modern organizations: competitive strategy, operational functionality, and technology.

The competitive strategies discussed include cost efficiency, differentiation, and market focus. The operational functionalities covered include supply chain management and marketing intelligence. The technologies utilized include cloud computing, the Internet of Things, and big data analytics.

The focus of the book is on the relative cause-and-effect relationships among the three core elements. In the first topic, the causal linkage is among emerging information technologies, competitive strategies, and supply chain management. In the second topic, the linkage is among the internet of things, marketing intelligence, and competitive strategies. In the third topic, the linkage is among competitive strategies, supply chain management, and big data analytics.

Each topic demonstrates theoretical backgrounds, research hypotheses, and empirical results with implications. Further references are also provided for each topic.

The theme of this book is highly related to some of the United Nations Sustainable Development Goals 2030 (SDGs 2030), in particular SDG 8—decent work and economic growth, SDG 9—industry, innovation, and infrastructure, and SDG12—responsible consumption and production.

I hope you enjoy reading this book.

Sustainable Organizations: The Role of Smart Technologies

About the author

Winston W. H. Weng is an independent researcher and writer. His research focuses on the sustainable development of the IT software industry. He has participated in a large number of research projects involving topics such as enterprise IT investments, IT outsourcing, business software, embedded software, open-source software, IT security, technology services, and the e-development of industries. Previously, he was a project manager working on topics including IT system development and maintenance services. He was also responsible for consultancy and training services for the e-development of corporations.

Chapter 1
Emerging information technologies and Competitive Strategies

Abstract

Recent advancements in information technology (IT) have invoked tremendous attention from both academics and industries. Emerging information technologies (EITs) such as cloud computing, big data analytics, and the Internet of Things not only serve as possible new tools for enterprise operations but also trigger impacts in management domains such as supply chain management. As managers and academics increasingly raise issues about the real value of EITs, the current authors question their direct and indirect performance effect. This study advanced research on the topic by investigating the role of critical mechanisms underlying the link between

EITs and supply chain performance (SCP). The current study constructed a research framework in which three strategy positions of firms, cost leadership, differentiation, and market focus, mediate the effect of EITs on SCP. An empirical survey was performed and an analysis of the data was conducted to test our hypotheses. The results confirmed the mediating role of competitive strategy in the link between EITs and SCP. Research contributions and managerial implications are elaborated.

Keywords: supply chain management; emerging information technology; competitive strategy; resource-based view; mediation effect

1. Introduction

Because of the high extent of recent globalisation, the meticulousness of enterprise internationalisation and business integration, and the rapid development of information technology (IT), business environments are changing tremendously. For enterprises, customers require an increasingly rapid response and fulfilment. To respond promptly to changing internal situations and external environments, enterprises must interact quickly with vendors of upper, middle, and lower streams through IT to form a highly efficient supply chain organisation.

The thriving development of various emerging ITs (EITs) such as cloud computing (Weng, 2021b; Weng & Lin, 2014a), big data analytics (Weng & Lin, 2013; Weng & Weng, 2013), and the Internet of Things (IoT) (Weng, 2021a; Weng & Lin, 2014c), is expected to affect enterprises' managerial performance, including supply chain performance (SCP). As the most noticed trends of recent IT development (Gartner, 2014, 2015; IDC, 2014, 2015; IEEE, 2014, 2015), these aforementioned EITs have attracted attention as possible sources of strategic advantages for firms (Porter & Heppelmann, 2014). Their economic and societal influence has also attracted the attention of governments and companies worldwide. EIT adoption provides strategic advantages for company managers and may even markedly change the future market (Iansiti & Lakhani, 2014). Therefore, aligning with the development trends of EITs has become critical for the development of companies' organisational strategies. Thus, this study focused on the managerial impact of innovative EITs (Gartner, 2015; IEEE, 2015; Porter & Heppelmann, 2014).

The recent trends of IT development centre on the evolution of EITs such as cloud computing, big data analytics, and the IoT (Gartner, 2015; IDC, 2015; IEEE, 2015). These EITs have also invoked tremendous attention from academics (Iansiti & Lakhani, 2014; Porter & Heppelmann, 2014). How firms react to the flourishing of EIT trends is a crucial issue. One major challenge is that the EITs are still under development. Consequently, their impacts on firms' performance have not been thoroughly realised and deserve further investigation.

Little rigorous research regarding the impact of EITs on firms' management activities and performance has been performed. Because supply chain management (SCM) is critical to a firm's operation and financial outcome (Qrunfleh & Tarafdar, 2014), this study focused on the influence of EITs on SCP.

This study explored the link between EITs and SCP and investigated the mediators in the link. The resource→strategy→performance scheme of competitive strategy (Day & Wensley, 1988; Venkatraman, 1989) was employed as a model of our research framework. Empirical data from quantitative survey questions were collected and analysed to realise the research hypotheses.

Through the research process and results, this study clarified the effect of EIT adoption intention on SCP and identified possible strategic mediators (Baron & Kenny, 1986; Jaccard, Wan, & Turrisi, 1990) of the effect.

2. Literature Review

2.1 Emerging Information Technology

Recently, EITs have attracted attention as possible sources for strategic advantages for firms (Porter & Heppelmann, 2014). Their economic and societal influence has also attracted the attention of governments and companies worldwide.

The most noticed EITs include cloud computing, big data analytics, and the IoT (Gartner, 2015; IDC, 2015; IEEE, 2015). Porter and Heppelmann (2014) described the potential power of these technologies in transforming enterprise competition.

(1) Cloud Computing

The innovation of cloud computing has had a major impact on the products, services, and business models in the IT software and hardware industries (Armbrust et al., 2010; Sultan, 2013; Vouk, 2008). Cloud computing has consequently become an emerging concept and technology that has drawn attention in the IT software and hardware industries. The scope of the cloud computing industry, as well as the fact that it spans both the enterprise and consumer markets, has led to much discussion on its future business potential (Graham, 2011; Iyer & Henderson, 2010; Katzan, 2009). Furthermore, cloud computing technology, as well as the new business models, products, and services that arise as a result, offer an emerging market that is well worth monitoring (Helland, 2013).

There are currently two main types of infrastructure management technology in cloud computing: virtualisation and software defined networking (SDN). Virtualisation software is commonly used in managing and deploying computing infrastructure such as virtualising server and storage devices. The technology has also been extended to fields in desktop virtualisation, application virtualisation, and Internet virtualisation (Sotomayor, Montero, Lorente, & Foster, 2009).

Furthermore, the rapid implementation of cloud-related infrastructure and flexible management of cloud data centres have gained relevance in cloud development. SDN is a new technology that reduces the requirement for hardware computing resources. H. Kim and Feamster (2013) discussed the concept and advancement of SDN as a promising technology for flexibly managing data centre networking devices.

(2) Big Data Analytics

"Big data" refers to large quantities of immediate, manifold structured and unstructured information. Big data analytics facilitates storing, transforming, transmitting, and analysing massive amounts of information (McAfee & Brynjolfsson, 2012; Weng & Lin, 2014b) for companies. It also provides advanced business analytics, develops business intelligence, and leads to gains in business value

(Chang, Kauffman, & Kwon, 2014; McAfee & Brynjolfsson, 2012).

The rapid growth of cloud computing, electronic commerce, social media, the IoT, and mobile devices has caused data volume to grow expansively and caused companies worldwide to pay attention to big data-related technology (Kwon, Lee, & Shin, 2014). Big data technology refers to the use of computing processes such as storing, transforming, streaming, transferring, and analysing to manage massive quantities of structural or nonstructural data that are dynamic and variable to attain business benefits (Jacobs, 2009). Big data technology is used to perform instant and complex analyses of massive amounts of dynamic data and to support companies' decision-making processes in a short period of time. The rise of big data has provided new opportunities for future information and communication technology industries and data scientists (Jelinek & Bergey, 2013).

Chen, Chiang, and Storey (2012) described the evolution of big data technology. They used business intelligence and analytics (BI&A) as a unified term and treated big data analytics as a related field. They argued that the evolution of big data technology is characterised by BI&A 1.0, BI&A 2.0, and BI&A 3.0. Data management and warehousing are considered the foundation of BI&A 1.0. BI&A 2.0 systems require the integration of scalable techniques in text mining, web mining, social network analysis, and spatial–temporal analysis with those existing database management system-based BI&A 1.0 systems. BI&A 3.0 integrates big data technology with mobile applications, such as mobile business intelligence, mobile and sensor-based content, location-aware analysis, person-centred analysis, context-relevant analysis, and mobile visualisations of data.

(3) Internet of Things

The IoT is a network for exchanging information in a mobile and ubiquitous manner (Agarwal & Brem, 2015; Iansiti & Lakhani, 2014; Porter & Heppelmann, 2014). To provide ubiquitous mobile computing, an infrastructure of wireless sensors and communication networks must be constructed first. Currently, various IoT networking infrastructures such as vehicular sensor networks (Agarwal & Brem, 2015; Atzori, Iera, & Morabito, 2010) are under development (Piran, Murthy, & Babu, 2011).

Near-field communication (Leong, Hew, Tan, & Ooi, 2013; Tan, Ooi, Chong, & Hew, 2014) evolved from radio-frequency identification (Ilie-Zudor, Kemény, van Blommestein, Monostori, & van der Meulen, 2011) and interconnection technology. In the past, noncontact chips have been produced as card applications. Recently, chips have been embedded into mobile devices for greater convenience. Consequently, mobile devices have become a payment tool that enables the downloading of and payment for services in any public setting and can also be used for exchanging data on mobile devices. This development extends the possible applications of smart, connected products and product clouds (Porter & Heppelmann, 2014).

2.2 Supply Chain Management

The goal of SCM is to facilitate the efficient and effective movement of products, services, finances, and information from a provider to a consumer. SCM not only is essential for the effective production, distribution, and logistical performance of current companies but also can influence their strategic position (Vijayasarathy, 2010). Understanding how firms can profit from their SCM is highly critical for both management practitioners and academics (DeGroote & Marx, 2013).

Prior research has characterised SCM as fundamentally reshaping enterprise competition and evolving into a part of a firm's new dominant logic (Wagner, Grosse-Ruyken, & Erhun, 2012). Researchers have argued that a firm's practices for leveraging the relationships in their supply chain can be fundamental to sustaining a competitive advantage in the market (Qrunfleh & Tarafdar, 2014).

2.3 Intention of Emerging Information Technology Adoption

Despite the continuing development of EITs, research regarding firms' adoption, impact analysis, and business strategy perspectives is still at its initial stage (Porter & Heppelmann, 2014).

The intention to adopt innovative technology is a result of the decision-making process of a firm. Gupta, Seetharaman, and Raj (2013) exploited possible adoption considerations concerning cloud computing technology. Factors that may influence adoption decisions regarding cloud computing, such as perception, attitude, and organisational culture, have been investigated (Lin & Chen, 2012; Sultan & van de Bunt-Kokhuis, 2012). Garrison, Kim, and Wakefield (2012) investigated possible success factors for deploying cloud computing. Cloud computing introduces a new risk into IT adoption. Subashini and Kavitha (2011) presented a survey of the different security risks that pose a threat to cloud computing.

Waller and Fawcett (2013) discussed considerations in adopting big data technology for firms. In their paper, data science, predictive analytics, and big data are collectively referred to as DPB. They argued that data science is the application of quantitative and qualitative methods to solve relevant problems and predict outcomes. Data scientists require extensive domain knowledge and a broad set of analytical skills. Predictive analytics is a subset of data science. Although predictive analytics is related to many long-standing quantitative approaches, it is distinct from them. Predictive analytics is used to quickly and inexpensively approximate relationships between variables while using deductive mathematical methods to draw conclusions. Chiang, Goes, and Stohr (2012) argued that the current state of the analytics software industry makes it difficult and cumbersome to conduct analyses without a clear perspective of the underlying systems and technologies. They advocated that BI&A should be interdisciplinary and be integrated with data management, database systems, data warehousing, data mining, natural language processing, text mining, network analysis, social networking, optimisation, and statistical analysis.

Cegielski, Allison Jones-Farmer, Wu, and Hazen (2012) reported that adoption intention is an appropriate indicator of actual adoption of EITs because of the relative newness of these technologies as a business tool. Thus, intention can be measured as an accurate proxy for actual adoption (Ke, Liu, Wei, Gu, & Chen, 2009). Furthermore, according to the resource-based view (RBV) of firms (Wernerfelt, 1984), the adoption intention concerning innovative technologies can be considered an intangible resource of firms (Kwon et al., 2014) . It is also related to organisational culture (Liu, Ke, Wei, Gu, & Chen, 2010).

3. Hypotheses Development

3.1 Impact of Information Technology on Supply Chain Performance

The possible impact of IT on SCP has been a crucial topic to both academics and practitioners. For enterprises, IT adoption facilitates and enhances information processing and exchange. The timely and accurate flow of information is a necessity for successful supply chain operations. Therefore, IT adoption in a supply chain is expected to produce positive results concerning performance. For example, Wu, Yeniyurt, Kim, and Cavusgil (2006) investigated the impact of IT on supply chain capabilities by drawing from the RBV of IT. The findings suggest that IT advancement and IT alignment can facilitate the development of supply chain capabilities.

Zhang, Pieter van Donk, and van der Vaart (2011) conducted a systematic review of the literature from the period 1995 to mid-2010 and found that a majority of papers confirmed a positive relationship between IT and SCP. More recently, DeGroote and Marx (2013) investigated the impact of IT on supply chain agility as measured by the ability to sense and respond to market changes. Their data were collected from supply chain executives at 193 U.S. manufacturing firms. The results suggested that IT improves a supply chain's ability to become aware of market changes by improving the adequacy, accuracy, accessibility, and timeliness of the information flows among members.

Furthermore, IT increases the supply chain's ability to respond to market changes by reducing the cost and improving the quality and timeliness of developing and executing coordinated plans to respond to market changes throughout the supply chain. Because the IT on which this study focused were EITs, the first hypothesis is as follows:

H1. EIT adoption intention is significantly associated with SCP.

3.2 Role of Competitive Strategy

Despite previous research results indicating significant impacts of IT on SCP, it can be argued that IT alone does not completely determine SCP. Business strategic thinking can also play a crucial role in SCP. For example, Huo, Qi, Wang, and Zhao (2014) surveyed 604 Chinese manufacturers and found that competitive strategies significantly influenced the effectiveness of supply chain practices, including internal, process, and product integration.

Porter's framework for competitive strategy is one of the most widely accepted business competition models (D. Miller, 1988). Porter's research in industrial economics suggested three generic competitive strategies for achieving above average rates of return: cost leadership, differentiation, and focus (Porter, 1980, 1985). He argued that to succeed in business, a firm must adopt one or more of these three generic competitive strategies and that a firm's strategic choice ultimately determines its competitiveness and profitability (A. Miller & Dess, 1993).

Regarding the research on firm performance, the RBV (Wernerfelt, 1984) of the firm attributes superior firm performance to firm resources. Firms build a competitive advantage by utilising unique sets of resources and strategies (Barney, 1991). Resources enable firms to conceive of and implement strategies, improving effectiveness (Barney, 1991). By contrast, strategies are the means by which firms relate to their environment (Porter, 1980, 1985). Strategies therefore affect the link between resources and performance (Edelman, Brush, & Manolova, 2005).

Day and Wensley (1988) extended the work of Porter (1980) by introducing the source→position→performance (SPP) framework of competitive advantage. In addition to acknowledging the performance impact of positional advantages in terms of superior customer value (e.g., differentiation) and lower relative costs (e.g., cost leadership), their framework embraces elements from the RBV (Wernerfelt, 1984) by arguing that organisational capabilities are the key sources of positional advantages.

Bharadwaj (2000) developed the concept of IT as an organisational resource by drawing on the RBV of the firm. The study empirically examined the association between IT as a resource and firm performance and found it to be positive and significant.

Koo, Koh, and Nam (2004) investigated Porter's competitive strategies in electronic virtual markets. In their research framework, firms' online business capability was considered a resource. Porter's framework of competitive strategies was applied to compare the market strategies of online firms and firms operating concurrently in the traditional and electronic markets. They also examined the connection between the firms' competitive strategies and business performance in electronic markets.

Edelman et al. (2005) provided a schematic representation of the resource→strategy→ performance model. They examined the relationships among firm resources, strategies, and performance in a cross-section of small firms. They used firm strategy as a mediating variable and reported that mediation test results evidenced the existence of a significant intervening mechanism (i.e., firm strategy) between the antecedent variable (i.e., firm resources) and the consequent variable (i.e., firm performance).

Reimann, Schilke, and Thomas (2009) drew from the SPP framework to build a research model in which two strategic positions of firms, differentiation and cost leadership, mediated the effect of customer relationship management (CRM) on firm performance. Their results revealed that CRM does not affect firm performance directly. Rather, the CRM–performance link is fully mediated by differentiation and cost leadership.

In this paper, EITs are viewed as sources of a competitive advantage for enhancing SCP (DeGroote & Marx, 2013; Dong, Xu, & Zhu, 2009; Vijayasarathy, 2010). The basic premise of our study is that the relationship between EIT adoption in the supply chain and SCP can be affected by the three strategic mediators of cost leadership, differentiation, and focus. Figure 1 shows this conceptual model.

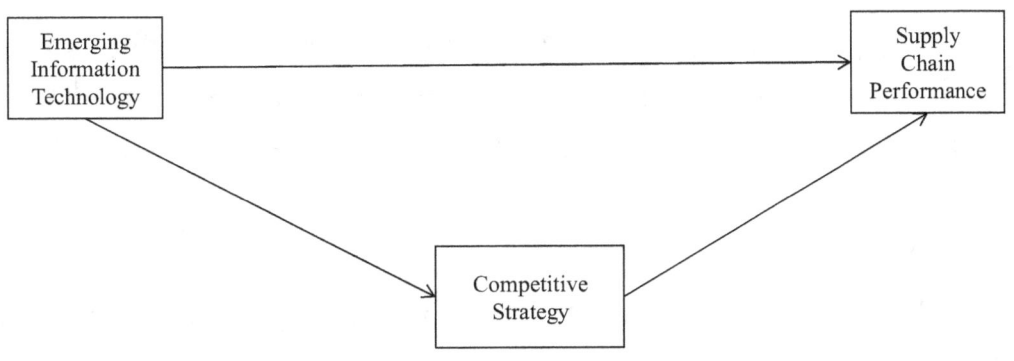

Figure 1　Conceptual model

(1) Cost Leadership

By using a cost leadership strategy, a firm can improve its competitive stance by lowering its manufacturing and marketing costs. A lower cost structure can improve profitability and the market share.

EITs have complicated the market dynamics, making it more difficult to predict how firms will compete in the market (Porter & Heppelmann, 2014). Few studies have examined how the relationship between technology adoption and cost leadership strategy influences how companies compete in a market. However, previous studies have shown that the integration of IT with supply chain management can reduce the cost of information exchange between parties in the supply chain and thus affect the SCP (Dong et al., 2009; Qrunfleh & Tarafdar, 2014).

We propose that EITs indirectly affect firm performance by increasing efficiency and driving down costs, implying that EITs significantly affect a firm's cost leadership position, leading to superior SCP. The following was thus hypothesised:

H2a: EIT adoption intention is significantly associated with cost leadership strategy position.

H2b: Cost leadership strategy position is significantly associated with SCP.

H2c: Cost leadership strategy position mediates the relationship between EIT adoption intention and SCP.

(2) Differentiation

A firm may pursue a strategic advantage by differentiating its products and services from those offered by its competitors. By providing unique and innovative products and services by using creative marketing, a firm can establish strong brand recognition and customer loyalty.

With a differentiation strategy, a firm seeks to be unique in the manner in which it offers products and services to customers, because this uniqueness leads to customers viewing the products and services as valuable (Porter, 1980). Porter and Millar (1985) further envisioned the potential of IT as a driving force behind differentiation strategies. Many believe that firms can also enhance value by creatively exploiting differentiated market segments and channels. Differentiation strategies in markets enable firms to charge premium prices for products and services deemed unique by customers (Porter, 2001).

Adopting EITs may enable a firm to obtain in-depth information about its suppliers and customers and then use this knowledge to adapt its offerings to meet the requirements of its supply chain operations more effectively than do its competitors. Therefore, EITs are linked to the business strategy of differentiation, which enables firms to achieve superior performance. This link is consistent with the SPP framework, with EITs as the source that enables firms to achieve a differentiated position that in turn drives firms' SCP (Day & Wensley, 1988).

H3a: EIT adoption intention is significantly associated with differentiation strategy position.

H3b: Differentiation strategy position is significantly associated with SCP.

H3c: Differentiation strategy position mediates the relationship between EIT adoption intention and SCP.

(3) Market Focus

An alternative strategy, focus, is generally held to be appropriate for small firms or entrepreneurs with few resources, because it enables them to compete with larger firms and position themselves on the basis of other strategic strengths (Wright, 1987).

With a focus strategy, a firm concentrates its efforts on a specific market segment (Porter, 1980). How this strategy performs in an IT-based market is not clear. Furthermore, no extensive empirical studies have examined the behaviour and performance of firms in the market competing on the basis of IT. Koo et al. (2004) examined Porter's competitive strategies in electronic virtual markets and found that online firms were inclined to adopt the differentiation strategy, whereas click-and-mortar firms preferred strategies based on the focus strategy. Both online firms and click-and-mortar firms are pioneer adopters of EITs such as cloud computing and big data analytics. Thus, our hypotheses are as follows:

H4a: EIT adoption intention is significantly associated with market focus strategy position.

H4b: Market focus strategy position is significantly associated with SCP.

H4c: Market focus strategy mediates the relationship between EIT adoption intention and SCP.

Based on our proposed hypotheses, the research framework is illustrated in Figure 2.

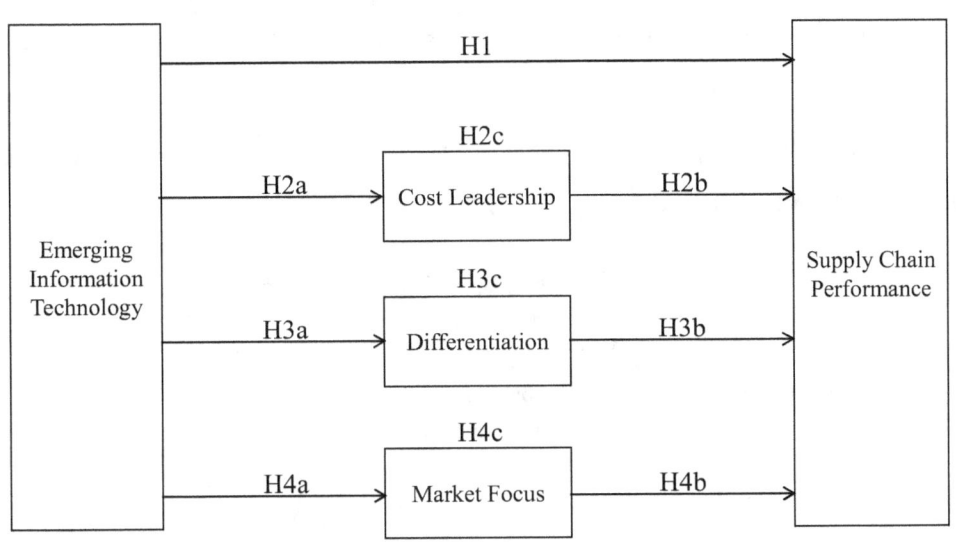

Figure 2　Research framework

4. Research Method

4.1 Survey Instrument

The survey instrument was developed using questions derived from the literature on EITs, Porter's competitive strategies, the resource→strategy→performance framework, and SCP discussed previously. We operationalised the study variables by using multi-item reflective measures on a 7-point scale (Jarvis et al. 2003).

Table 1 summarises the independent and dependent variables, which are further elaborated as follows.

Table 1   Research variables

Construct	Operational Definition	Supporting Literature
Emerging information technology	A firm's intention to adopt the emerging information technology	Armbrust et al. (2010) Cegielski et al. (2012)
Cost leadership	A firm's posture of competition based on lower cost of operation and resource relative to the firm's competitors.	Koo et al. (2004) Reimann et al. (2009) Oltra and Luisa Flor (2010)
Differentiation	A firm's ability to compete by being unique within their industry in a number of perspectives.	Koo et al. (2004) Reimann et al. (2009)
Focus	A firm's ability to compete by targeting specific groups of buyers, product lines, product lifecycle, or geographic areas.	Koo et al. (2004) E. Kim, Nam, and Stimpert (2004)

Supply chain performance	A firm's assessment of the efficiency and effectiveness of its supply chain.	Wu et al. (2006) Vijayasarathy (2010) DeGroote and Marx (2013) Qrunfleh and Tarafdar (2014)

(1) Emerging Information Technology Construct

The EIT construct was measured using five items that reflect a firm's intention to adopt the technologies. These items were based on technology forecast reports by renowned market research institutions and academic literature. Global market research firms such as Gartner (Gartner, 2014, 2015) and IDC (IDC, 2014, 2015) publish top technology trend predictions annually. Academic societies such as the IEEE Computer Society also announce the top 10 annual technology trends (IEEE, 2014, 2015). In addition, this study focused on the EIT items in the structure of the "new technology stack" depicted by Porter and Heppelmann (2014).

We chose to measure the adoption intention rather than actual adoption of the EITs because of the relative newness of them as a business tool. The relevant literature provides extensive support for the notion that intention, when placed in context with respect to time, is an accurate proxy for measuring action (Cegielski et al., 2012).

(2) Cost Leadership Construct

The cost leadership construct was measured using three items that reflect the extent to which a firm deploys a cost-oriented strategy. First, cost leadership refers to the generation of higher margins than those of competitors by achieving lower operation costs. Firms with a cost leadership strategy often have highly stable product lines and a strong emphasis on profit and budget controls (D. Miller, 1988). Second, cost leadership is often reflected in price competitiveness (Koo et al., 2004). The third item was the economic scale. A firm can gain a cost advantage through economies of scale or superior manufacturing processes (Porter, 1980, 1985). Generally, larger firms with greater access to resources are more likely to take advantage of cost leadership strategies, whereas smaller firms are often forced to compete using highly differentiated products and services in a niche market (Wright, 1987).

(3) Differentiation Construct

The differentiation construct was measured using four items that reflect the extent to which a firm deploys a differentiation strategy.

First, differentiation entails being unlike or distinct from competitors, for example, by providing superior information, prices, distribution channels, and prestige to the customer (Porter, 1980). Differentiation prevents a business from competitive rivalry, insulating it from competitive forces that reduce margins (Phillips et al. 1983).

Extending Porter's competitive strategy framework, Miller distinguished differentiation strategies based on innovation from those based on operational and marketing efficiency (D. Miller, 1988; Wright, 1987). These categories form two items included in the construct.

Differentiation strategies based on innovation can create a dynamic market environment or a distinct business model in which it is difficult for competitors and customers to predict and react. This unpredictability can give the innovator a substantial advantage over its competitors (D. Miller, 1987). We further distinguished innovation into new markets and new business models.

(4) Market Focus Construct

We based our measure of the market focus construct on the research constructs of Koo et al. (2004) and Laosirihongthong, Tan, and Kannan (2010).

A firm can obtain a strategic advantage by specialising and focusing on a niche market instead of competing broadly in the whole market. The choice of the market segment to focus on can be based on dimensions such as prices, customer groups, product functions, and geographical location. Isoherranen (2011) evaluated the characteristics of technology orientation, market orientation, customer focus, and product focus in a case business. We measured the focus construct by using four items which reflect four market and product segments.

(5) Supply Chain Performance Construct

SCP served as the dependent variable and was measured using seven items. Respondents rated their SCP over the past few years relative to that of their competitors on a 7-point scale.

Beamon (1999) proposed a framework for measuring SCP. The framework included the measurement of resources, output, and flexibility as the strategic goals of SCM. The key measuring variables included cost, activity time, customer responsiveness, and flexibility. Neely, Gregory, and Platts (1995) discussed design issues regarding SCP measurement systems. The metrics and measures were also discussed in the context of supply chain processes such as planning, sourcing, manufacturing or assembling, and delivery to the customer (Gunasekaran, Patel, & McGaughey, 2004; Gunasekaran, Patel, & Tirtiroglu, 2001).

We focused on supply chain effectiveness (the achievement of specific objectives) and efficiency (the means by which specific objectives were attained), which have been recognised as direct and observable goals of SCM practice. Firms in a supply chain achieve operational efficiency and effectiveness by lowering costs, reducing inventory, promoting flexibility, ensuring on-time deliveries, and minimising shortages of critical resources. These objectives relate to both parties in a buyer–supplier relationship, and therefore, can represent the performance of the overall supply chain.

Table 2 presents the items used to measure each of the independent and dependent variables.

Table 2 Items used in the survey

Variable	Item
Emerging information technology adoption intention (1 – to no extent; 4 – to some extent; 7 – to a great extent)	
	EIT1: cloud computing
	EIT2: big data analytics
	EIT3: internet of things
Cost Leadership strategy position (1 – strongly disagree; 7 – strongly agree)	
	CL1: Developing products or services with lower cost
	CL2: Delivering products or services with lower price
	CL3: Providing products or services in large quantity or scale
Differentiation strategy position (1 – strongly disagree; 7 – strongly agree)	
	DF1: Differentiating products and services based on operational efficiency
	DF2: Differentiating products and services based on innovation
	DF3: Delivering products or services with superior functionality in current market
	DF4: Delivering products or services with innovative business model

Market Focus strategy position
(1 – strongly disagree; 7 – strongly agree)

    MF1: Focusing in a niche market segment

    MF2: Focusing in first to market position

    MF3: Focusing in market position as a fast follower

    MF4: Focusing in a mature market segment

Supply Chain Performance
(1 – greatly below average; 4 – average; 7 – greatly above average)

    SCP1: Delivering products or services on time

    SCP2: Reducing lead time

    SCP3: Responding to changes of customer requirement

    SCP4: Avoiding lack of critical resources

    SCP5: Inventory and logistics flexibility

    SCP6: Reducing cost of the whole supply chain management

    SCP7: Reducing inventory cost

4.2 Sample and Data Collection

Empirical data for testing the hypothesised relationships were obtained by conducting a survey of large Taiwanese companies. An online questionnaire developed in accordance with Table 2 was implemented as the survey instrument. It was pretested in an iterative manner among a sample of 15 executives and supply chain managers. The questionnaire items were revised on the basis of the results of the expert interviews and refined through rigorous pretesting to establish content validity. The pretesting focused on instrument clarity, question wording, and validity. During the pretesting, members of the testing sample were invited to comment on the questions and wording of the questionnaire. The comments of these respondents then provided a basis for revisions to the construct measures.

After the pretesting and revision, data were collected through an online survey of supply chain executives and managers. China Credit Information Service, Ltd. provided comprehensive data on the 5,000 largest companies in Taiwan. We randomly selected 2,300 firms as the sample of this study.

Table 3 shows the profile of the final sample list. The list for this research provides the names, addresses, and email addresses of the 2,300 randomly chosen members. Survey invitations were sent to the firms in the list by email. Follow-up letters were sent approximately 1 month after the initial mailing. In total, 201 valid questionnaires were obtained, with a response rate of 8.74%.

Table 3 Profile of the final sampling firms

Industry	Frequency	%
High-tech manufacturing	54	27%
Other manufacturing	37	18%
IT and Telecom services	43	21%
Other services	33	16%
Retail and wholesale	34	17%
Total	201	100%

5. Results

Our goal was to investigate the impact of EITs on SCP, mediated by a firm's competitive strategy position. The empirical results were expected to demonstrate that EITs, such as cloud computing, big data, and the IoT (Iansiti & Lakhani, 2014; Porter & Heppelmann, 2014), influence the SCP by, for example, reducing cost, increasing flexibility, and shortening time spent on tasks. The results were also expected to verify the mediating role of Porter's theory of generic strategy (Porter, 1980, 1985) on the link between EITs and SCP. Finally, the results were used to test the SPP framework of competitive strategy (Day & Wensley, 1988; Venkatraman, 1989).

5.1 Reliability and Validity

The reliability of the survey instrument was tested by using Cronbach's alpha (Cronbach, 1951) to assess the internal consistency of the EIT, cost leadership, differentiation, market focus, and SCP constructs. Cronbach's alpha tests the interrelationship among the items composing a construct to determine if the items measure a single construct. Nunnally and Bernstein (1994) recommended a threshold alpha value of .7. Cicchetti et al. (2011) suggested the following reliability guidelines for determining significance: $\alpha < .70$ (unacceptable), $.70 \leq \alpha < .80$ (fair), $.80 \leq \alpha < .90$ (good), and $\alpha > .90$ (excellent).

Content validity (Straub, 1989) refers to the extent to which the instrument measures what it is designed to measure. Most of the measures used in the study were adopted from relevant studies. Although basing the study on the established literature provided a considerable level of validity, the study's validity was further improved by pretesting the instrument on a panel of experts comprising 15 executives and supply chain managers.

To assess convergent and discriminant validity, the items that were used to measure the EIT, cost leadership, differentiation, market focus, and SCP constructs were subjected to principal components analysis with varimax rotation. The Bartlett test of sphericity and the Kaiser–Meyer–Olkin measure of sampling adequacy were conducted to ensure that the sample was satisfactory and confirm the appropriateness of proceeding with further data analysis.

Table 4 summarises the descriptive statistics and results of the reliability and validity tests. The reliability of the instrument was examined using composite reliability estimates by employing Cronbach's α. All the coefficients exceeded Nunnally's recommended level (0.70) of internal consistency (Cicchetti et al., 2011; Nunnally & Bernstein, 1994). In addition, factor analysis was performed to confirm the construct validity. The results supported the constructs of our research model.

Table 4 Descriptive statistics and reliability and validity test

Construct	Item	Mean	SD	Cronbach's alpha	Cronbach's alpha if item deleted	Factor loading on single factor
Emerging Information Technology	EIT1	4.58	1.233	0.872	0.858	0.866
	EIT2	4.32	1.438		0.774	0.918
	EIT3	4.17	1.307		0.815	0.893
Cost Leadership	CL1	4.46	1.414	0.719	0.724	0.732
	CL2	3.72	1.521		0.596	0.824
	CL3	3.60	1.460		0.557	0.842
Differentiation	DF1	4.55	1.371	0.905	0.893	0.854
	DF2	4.39	1.375		0.857	0.921
	DF3	4.31	1.579		0.889	0.866
	DF4	4.21	1.456		0.870	0.895
Market Focus	MF1	4.52	1.379	0.852	0.806	0.839
	MF2	4.31	1.485		0.812	0.834
	MF3	4.32	1.311		0.835	0.792
	MF4	4.22	1.372		0.792	0.864
Supply Chain Performance	SCP1	4.51	1.460	0.931	0.926	0.795
	SCP2	4.61	1.330		0.918	0.858
	SCP3	4.94	1.338		0.917	0.866
	SCP4	4.55	1.330		0.921	0.832
	SCP5	4.55	1.396		0.917	0.868
	SCP6	4.42	1.465		0.922	0.828
	SCP7	4.64	1.338		0.920	0.847

5.2 Construct Correlation

Table 5 summarises the correlations among different factors. We also assessed discriminant validity on the basis of the construct correlation that Campbell and Fiske (1959) proposed. The tests indicated acceptable results with respect to discriminant validity.

Table 5　Construct correlation

Construct		EIT	CL	DF	MF	SCP
Emerging Information Technology	EIT	1				
Low Cost	CL	0.343**	1			
Differentiation	DF	0.352**	0.647**	1		
Market Focus	MF	0.419**	0.663**	0.774**	1	
Supply Chain Performance	SCP	0.377**	0.622**	0.650**	0.759**	1

*p < 0.05, **p < 0.01, *** p < 0.001

5.3 Tests of Hypotheses

Table 6 summarises the test results regarding the parameter estimates of the total effects. The results supported the hypotheses that EIT adoption intention and competitive strategy position are positively related to SCP.

Table 6 Tests for total effects

Hypothesis		Coefficient	p-value	Test Result
H1	EIT → SCP	0.362***	0.000	Supported
H2a	EIT → CL	0.324***	0.000	Supported
H2b	CL → SCP	0.622***	0.000	Supported
H3a	EIT → DF	0.356***	0.000	Supported
H3b	DF → SCP	0.650***	0.000	Supported
H4a	EIT → MF	0.421***	0.000	Supported
H4b	MF → SCP	0.759***	0.000	Supported

*p < 0.05, **p < 0.01, *** p < 0.001

Table 7 summarises the test results concerning mediation. The results show that introducing the mediating variables reduced the coefficient of the H1 link, and the direct effect of EITs on SCP was nonsignificant. This established a complete mediation effect.

Table 7 Tests for mediation

	Path	Coefficient	p-value	Effect	VIF	Mediation
H1 total	EIT → SCP	0.362***	0.000	Total	1	
H1 direct	EIT → SCP	0.040	0.427	Direct	1.221	Complete
H2c	EIT → CL → SCP	0.071***	0.000	Indirect	1.867	
H3c	EIT → DF → SCP	-0.031	0.333	Indirect	4.117	
H4c	EIT → MF → SCP	0.283***	0.000	Indirect	4.473	

*p < 0.05, **p < 0.01, *** p < 0.001

6. Discussion and Conclusions

This study investigated the impact of EITs on SCP, mediated by a firm's competitive strategy position. Managerial implications and possible avenues for further research are elaborated as follows.

6.1 Managerial Implications

Supporting the research hypotheses, the critical insight we obtained from our empirical results is that the link between EITs and SCP was completely mediated by the strategies of firms. In other words, the link between EITs and SCP is not direct, but rather indirect. By adopting a mediational framework in this study, we isolated the specific effects by which EITs are linked to SCP. To the best of our knowledge, this is the first empirical study to investigate critical mediators concerning the IT and performance link, and to examine EITs in the context of competitive strategies.

The second significant observation is the difference in the effects of the three strategies. For the cost leadership and market focus strategies, the indirect effects were positive and significant. However, for the differentiation strategy, the indirect effect was nonsignificant. This finding suggests that differentiation strategy plays a unique role in competition and has less of an impact on the link between EIT adoption and SCP. Furthermore, the market focus strategy, which is employed by many innovative and start-up firms, has the highest effect on the link.

From the SPP (Day & Wensley, 1988) perspective, we assert that EITs are the sources of strategic positions, which in turn improve firm SCP. However, these specific strategic positions are cost leadership and market focus, but not differentiation.

6.2 Study Limitations

Although this study reported meaningful implications regarding the development of multidimensional measures of factors that influence SCP, we realise that the validity of an instrument cannot be firmly established on the basis of a single study. In this study, all data used for tests were collected from firms located in Taiwan. Taiwan is a relatively efficient and competitive arena for accepting new IT, but it has its own industry characteristics. In particular, manufacturing and retail industries are the dominant industries in Taiwan. Therefore, SCM practitioners and academics are suggested to interpret our findings as a guide model rather than generalising our measures to all emerging technologies.

6.3 Further Research

As stated previously, further research efforts which focus on accumulating more empirical evidence for assessing and validating empirical data are necessary to overcome the limitations of the present study. Such research is required to address how other variables relate to SCP. Wearable interface technology, for example, has received inadequate attention from management information systems and technology innovation theories. Further research could also investigate the relative importance of the factors affecting each stage of the supply chain process. These efforts should involve studies identifying the organisational capabilities which affect business operation, information processing, and decision support. In addition, special attention could be focused on data collected in various industries or specific contexts over an extended period of time. The analysis of this data may enable conclusions to be drawn about more generalised relationships among technology, strategy, and performance.

References

Agarwal, N., & Brem, A. (2015). Strategic business transformation through technology convergence: implications from General Electrics industrial internet initiative. *International Journal of Technology Management, 67*(2/3/4), 196-214.

Armbrust, M., Stoica, I., Zaharia, M., Fox, A., Griffith, R., Joseph, A. D., . . . Rabkin, A. (2010). A view of cloud computing. *Communications of the ACM, 53*(4), 50. doi:10.1145/1721654.1721672

Atzori, L., Iera, A., & Morabito, G. (2010). The Internet of Things: A survey. *Computer Networks, 54*(15), 2787-2805. doi:10.1016/j.comnet.2010.05.010

Barney, J. (1991). Firm Resources and Sustained Competitive Advantage *Journal of Management 17*(1), 99-120. doi:10.1177/014920639101700108

Baron, R. M., & Kenny, D. A. (1986). The moderator–mediator variable distinction in social psychological research: Conceptual, strategic, and statistical considerations. *Journal of Personality and Social Psychology, 51*(6), 1173-1182. doi:10.1037/0022-3514.51.6.1173

Beamon, B. M. (1999). Measuring supply chain performance. *International Journal of Operations & Production Management, 19*(3), 275-292. doi:10.1108/01443579910249714

Bharadwaj, A. S. (2000). A resource-based perspective on information technology capability and firm performance: an empirical investigation. *MIS Quarterly, 24*(1), 169-196.

Campbell, D., T., & Fiske, D., W. (1959). Convergent and discriminant validation by the multitrait-multimethod matrix. *Psychological Bulletin, 56*(2), 81-105.

Cegielski, C. G., Allison Jones-Farmer, L., Wu, Y., & Hazen, B. T. (2012). Adoption of cloud computing technologies in supply chains. *The International Journal of Logistics*

Management, 23(2), 184-211. doi:10.1108/09574091211265350

Chang, R. M., Kauffman, R. J., & Kwon, Y. (2014). Understanding the paradigm shift to computational social science in the presence of big data. *Decision Support Systems, 63*, 67-80. doi:10.1016/j.dss.2013.08.008

Chen, H., Chiang, R. H. L., & Storey, V. C. (2012). Business Intelligence and Analytics: From Big Data to Big Impact. *MIS Quarterly, 36*(4), 1165-1188.

Chiang, R. H. L., Goes, P., & Stohr, E. A. (2012). Business Intelligence and Analytics Education, and Program Development. *ACM Transactions on Management Information Systems, 3*(3), 1-13. doi:10.1145/2361256.2361257

Cicchetti, D. V., Koenig, K., Klin, A., Volkmar, F. R., Paul, R., & Sparrow, S. (2011). From Bayes through marginal utility to effect sizes: a guide to understanding the clinical and statistical significance of the results of autism research findings. *J Autism Dev Disord, 41*(2), 168-174. doi:10.1007/s10803-010-1035-6

Cronbach, L. (1951). Coefficient alpha and the internal structure of tests. *Psychometrika, 16*(3), 297-334. doi:10.1007/BF02310555

Day, G. S., & Wensley, R. (1988). Assessing advantage: a framework for diagnosing competitive superiority. *Journal of Marketing, 52*(2), 1-20.

DeGroote, S. E., & Marx, T. G. (2013). The impact of IT on supply chain agility and firm performance: An empirical investigation. *International Journal of Information Management, 33*(6), 909-916. doi:10.1016/j.ijinfomgt.2013.09.001

Dong, S., Xu, S. X., & Zhu, K. X. (2009). Research Note—Information Technology in Supply Chains: The Value of IT-Enabled Resources Under Competition. *Information Systems Research, 20*(1), 18-32. doi:10.1287/isre.1080.0195

Edelman, L. F., Brush, C. G., & Manolova, T. (2005). Co-alignment in the resource–performance relationship: strategy as mediator. *Journal of Business Venturing, 20*(3), 359-383. doi:10.1016/j.jbusvent.2004.01.004

Garrison, G., Kim, S., & Wakefield, R. L. (2012). Success factors for deploying cloud computing. *Communications of the ACM, 55*(9), 62. doi:10.1145/2330667.2330685

Gartner. (2014). The Top 10 Strategic Technology Trends for 2014. Retrieved from https://www.gartner.com/doc/2667526

Gartner. (2015). Research Guide: The Top 10 Strategic Technology Trends for 2015. Retrieved from https://www.gartner.com/doc/2966917

Graham, M. (2011). Cloud Collaboration: Peer-Production and the Engineering of the internet. 67-83. doi:10.1007/978-90-481-9920-4_5

Gunasekaran, A., Patel, C., & McGaughey, R. E. (2004). A framework for supply chain performance measurement.

International Journal of Production Economics, 87(3), 333-347. doi:10.1016/j.ijpe.2003.08.003

Gunasekaran, A., Patel, C., & Tirtiroglu, E. (2001). Performance measures and metrics in a supply chain environment. *International Journal of Operations & Production Management, 21*(1/2), 71-87. doi:10.1108/01443570110358468

Gupta, P., Seetharaman, A., & Raj, J. R. (2013). The usage and adoption of cloud computing by small and medium businesses. *International Journal of Information Management, 33*(5), 861-874. doi:10.1016/j.ijinfomgt.2013.07.001

Helland, P. (2013). Condos and clouds. *Communications of the ACM, 56*(1), 50. doi:10.1145/2398356.2398374

Huo, B., Qi, Y., Wang, Z., & Zhao, X. (2014). The impact of supply chain integration on firm performance. *Supply Chain Management: An International Journal, 19*(4), 369-384. doi:10.1108/scm-03-2013-0096

Iansiti, M., & Lakhani, K. R. (2014). Digital Ubiquity - How Connections, Sensors, and Data Are Revolutionizing Business. *Harvard Business Review, November*, 91-99.

IDC. (2014). *IDC Predictions 2014: Battles for Dominance — and Survival — on the 3rd Platform* (244606). Retrieved from

IDC. (2015). *IDC Predictions 2015: Accelerating Innovation — and Growth — on the 3rd Platform* (252700). Retrieved from

IEEE. (2014). Top Technology Trends for 2014. Retrieved from http://www.computer.org/portal/web/membership/Top-10-Tech-Trends-in-2014

IEEE. (2015). Top Technology Trends for 2015. Retrieved from http://www.computer.org/portal/web/membership/Top-Tech-Trends-for-2015

Ilie-Zudor, E., Kemény, Z., van Blommestein, F., Monostori, L., & van der Meulen, A. (2011). A survey of applications and requirements of unique identification systems and RFID techniques. *Computers in Industry, 62*(3), 227-252. doi:10.1016/j.compind.2010.10.004

Isoherranen, V. (2011). Analysis of Strategy Focus vs. Market Share in the Mobile Phone Case Business. *Technology and Investment, 02*(02), 134-141. doi:10.4236/ti.2011.22014

Iyer, B., & Henderson, J. C. (2010). Preparing for the Future: Understanding the Seven Capabilities of Cloud Computing. *MIS Quarterly Executive, 9*(2), 117-131.

Jaccard, J., Wan, C. K., & Turrisi, R. (1990). The Detection and Interpretation of Interaction Effects Between Gontinuous Variables in Multiple Regression. *Multivariate Behavioral Research, 25*(4), 467-478.

Jacobs, A. (2009). The pathologies of big data. *Communications of the ACM, 52*(8), 36. doi:10.1145/1536616.1536632

Jelinek, M., & Bergey, P. (2013). Innovation as the strategic driver of sustainability: big data knowledge for profit and survival. *IEEE Engineering Management Review, 41*(2), 14-22. doi:10.1109/emr.2013.2259978

Katzan, H. J. (2009). Cloud Software Service: Concepts, Technology, Economics. *Service Science, 1*(4), 256-269.

Ke, W., Liu, H., Wei, K. K., Gu, J., & Chen, H. (2009). How do mediated and non-mediated power affect electronic supply chain management system adoption? The mediating effects of trust and institutional pressures. *Decision Support Systems, 46*(4), 839-851. doi:10.1016/j.dss.2008.11.008

Kim, E., Nam, D.-i., & Stimpert, J. L. (2004). The applicability of Porter's generic strategies in the digital age: assumptions, conjectures, and suggestions. *Journal of Management, 30*(5), 569-589. doi:10.1016/j.jm.2003.12.001

Kim, H., & Feamster, N. (2013). Improving Network Management with Software Defined Networking. *IEEE Communications Magazine, February*, 114-119.

Koo, C. M., Koh, C. E., & Nam, K. (2004). An Examination of Porter's Competitive Strategies in Electronic Virtual Markets: A Comparison of Two On-line Business Models. *International Journal of Electronic Commerce, 9*(1), 163-180.

Kwon, O., Lee, N., & Shin, B. (2014). Data quality management, data usage experience and acquisition intention of big data analytics. *International Journal of Information Management, 34*(3), 387-394. doi:10.1016/j.ijinfomgt.2014.02.002

Laosirihongthong, T., Tan, K. C., & Kannan, V. R. (2010). The impact of market focus on operations practices. *International Journal of Production Research, 48*(20), 5943-5961. doi:10.1080/00207540903232797

Leong, L.-Y., Hew, T.-S., Tan, G. W.-H., & Ooi, K.-B. (2013). Predicting the determinants of the NFC-enabled mobile credit card acceptance: A neural networks approach. *Expert Systems with Applications, 40*(14), 5604-5620. doi:10.1016/j.eswa.2013.04.018

Lin, A., & Chen, N.-C. (2012). Cloud computing as an innovation: Percepetion, attitude, and adoption. *International Journal of Information Management, 32*(6), 533-540. doi:10.1016/j.ijinfomgt.2012.04.001

Liu, H., Ke, W., Wei, K. K., Gu, J., & Chen, H. (2010). The role of institutional pressures and organizational culture in the firm's intention to adopt internet-enabled supply chain management systems. *Journal of Operations Management, 28*(5), 372-384. doi:10.1016/j.jom.2009.11.010

McAfee, A., & Brynjolfsson, E. (2012). Big Data- The Management Revolution. *Harvard Business Review, October*, 1-9.

Miller, A., & Dess, G. G. (1993). Assessing Porter's (1980) model in terms of generalizability, ccuracy, and simplicity *Journal of Management Studies, 30*(4), 553-585.

Miller, D. (1987). The structural and environmental correlates of business strategy. *Strategic Management Journal, 8*(1), 55-76.

Miller, D. (1988). Relating porter's business strategies to environment and structure: analysis and performance implications. *Academy of Management Journal, 31*(2), 280-308.

Neely, A., Gregory, M., & Platts, K. (1995). Performance measurement system design. *International Journal of Operations & Production Management, 15*(4), 80-116. doi:10.1108/01443579510083622

Nunnally, J. C., & Bernstein, I. H. (1994). *Psychometric theory* (3 ed.). New York: McGraw-Hill.

Oltra, M. J., & Luisa Flor, M. (2010). The moderating effect of business strategy on the relationship between operations strategy and firms' results. *International Journal of Operations & Production Management, 30*(6), 612-638. doi:10.1108/01443571011046049

Piran, M. J., Murthy, G. R., & Babu, G. P. (2011). Vehicular Ad Hoc and Sensor Networks: Principals and Challenges. *International Journal of Ad hoc, Sensor & Ubiquitous Computing, 2*(2), 38-49. doi:10.5121/ijasuc.2011.2204

Porter, M. E. (1980). *Competitive Strategy*. New York: Free Press.

Porter, M. E. (1985). *Competitive Advantage*. New York: Free Press.

Porter, M. E. (2001). Strategy and the Internet. *Harvard Business Review, 79*(2), 63-78.

Porter, M. E., & Heppelmann, J. E. (2014). How Smart, Connected Products Are Transforming Competition. *Harvard Business Review, November*, 64-88.

Porter, M. E., & Millar, V. E. (1985). How information gives you competitive advantage. *Harvard Business Review, 63*(4), 61-78.

Qrunfleh, S., & Tarafdar, M. (2014). Supply chain information systems strategy: Impacts on supply chain performance and firm performance. *International*

Journal of Production Economics, 147, 340-350. doi:10.1016/j.ijpe.2012.09.018

Reimann, M., Schilke, O., & Thomas, J. S. (2009). Customer relationship management and firm performance: the mediating role of business strategy. *Journal of the Academy of Marketing Science, 38*(3), 326-346. doi:10.1007/s11747-009-0164-y

Sotomayor, B., Montero, R. S., Lorente, I. M., & Foster, I. (2009). Virtual infrastructure management in private and hybrid clouds. *IEEE Internet Computing, 13*(5), 14-22.

Straub, D. W. (1989). Validating instruments in MIS research. *MIS Quarterly, 13*(2), 147-169.

Subashini, S., & Kavitha, V. (2011). A survey on security issues in service delivery models of cloud computing. *Journal of Network and Computer Applications, 34*(1), 1-11. doi:10.1016/j.jnca.2010.07.006

Sultan, N. (2013). Cloud computing: A democratizing force? *International Journal of Information Management, 33*(5), 810-815. doi:10.1016/j.ijinfomgt.2013.05.010

Sultan, N., & van de Bunt-Kokhuis, S. (2012). Organisational culture and cloud computing: coping with a disruptive innovation. *Technology Analysis & Strategic Management, 24*(2), 167-179. doi:10.1080/09537325.2012.647644

Tan, G. W.-H., Ooi, K.-B., Chong, S.-C., & Hew, T.-S. (2014). NFC mobile credit card: The next frontier of mobile payment? *Telematics and Informatics, 31*(2), 292-307. doi:10.1016/j.tele.2013.06.002

Venkatraman, N. (1989). The concept of fit in strategy research - Toward verbal and statistical correspondence. *Academy of Management Review, 14*(3), 423-444.

Vijayasarathy, L. R. (2010). An investigation of moderators of the link between technology use in the supply chain and supply chain performance. *Information & Management, 47*(7-8), 364-371. doi:10.1016/j.im.2010.08.004

Vouk, M. A. (2008). Cloud Computing – Issues, Research and Implementations. *Journal of Computing and Information Technology, 16*(4), 235-246. doi:10.2498/cit.1001391

Wagner, S. M., Grosse-Ruyken, P. T., & Erhun, F. (2012). The link between supply chain fit and financial performance of the firm. *Journal of Operations Management, 30*(4), 340-353. doi:10.1016/j.jom.2012.01.001

Waller, M. A., & Fawcett, S. E. (2013). Data Science, Predictive Analytics, and Big Data: A Revolution That Will Transform Supply Chain Design and Management. *Journal of Business Logistics, 34*(2), 77-84.

Weng, W. H. (2021a). *Influential components for the sustainability of IoT-enabled smart systems: A hierarchical analysis.* Paper presented at the Third IEEE Eurasia Conference on Biomedical Engineering, Healthcare and Sustainability 2021 (IEEE ECBIOS 2021), Tainan, Taiwan.

Weng, W. H. (2021b). *Prioritizing critical cloud services for disastrous pandemics: A media richness perspective.*

Paper presented at the Proceedings of the Twenty-First International Conference on Electronic Business (ICEB 2021), Nanjing, China.

Weng, W. H., & Lin, W. T. (2013). A Big Data technology foresight study with scenario planning approach. *International Journal of Innovation in Management, 1*(2), 41-52.

Weng, W. H., & Lin, W. T. (2014a). Development assessment and strategy planning in cloud computing industry. *International Journal of Electronic Commerce Studies, 5*(2), 257-266. doi:10.7903/ijecs.1158

Weng, W. H., & Lin, W. T. (2014b). Development trends and strategy planning in big data industry. *Contemporary Management Research, 10*(3).

Weng, W. H., & Lin, W. T. (2014c). A scenario analysis of wearable interface technology foresight. *AIS Electronic Library (AISeL)*.

Weng, W. H., & Weng, W. T. (2013). *Forecast of development trends in big data industry*. Paper presented at the

Proceedings of the Institute of Industrial Engineers Asian Conference 2013, Taipei, Taiwan.

Wernerfelt, B. (1984). A Resource-based View of the Firm. *Strategic .Management Journal, 5*, 171-180.

Wright, P. (1987). A Refinement of Porter's generic strategies. *Strategic Management Journal, 8*, 93-101.

Wu, F., Yeniyurt, S., Kim, D., & Cavusgil, S. T. (2006). The impact of information technology on supply chain capabilities and firm performance: A resource-based view. *Industrial Marketing Management, 35*(4), 493-504. doi:10.1016/j.indmarman.2005.05.003

Zhang, X., Pieter van Donk, D., & van der Vaart, T. (2011). Does ICT influence supply chain management and performance? *International Journal of Operations & Production Management, 31*(11), 1215-1247. doi:10.1108/01443571111178501

Chapter 2
Internet of Things and Marketing Intelligence

Abstract

Innovative developments in the Internet of Things (IoT) have invoked tremendous attention from both academics and industries. Studies suggest that IoT not only serves as an innovative tool for enterprise operations but also triggers impacts on business performance. As researchers increasingly raise issues about the business value of IoT, this study examines its direct and indirect managerial effects by investigating the link between IoT and business strategy. Referring to the organizational capability perspective, this study constructed a research framework in which marketing intelligence capability mediates the effect of IoT capability on business strategy formation. An empirical survey was performed and an analysis of the data was conducted to test the hypotheses. The results confirmed the mediating role of marketing intelligence capability in the link between IoT capability and business strategy formation. Discussions with managerial implications are then elaborated.

Keywords: Internet of Things, marketing intelligence, business strategy, organizational capability

1. Introduction

Recent development of the extensive globalization, the meticulousness of enterprise internationalization and business integration, and the rapid development of innovative technologies have caused business environments to change rapidly and enormously. For enterprises, customers require an increasingly fast response and personalized fulfillment. To respond effectively to changing internal situations and external environments, a firm must interact closely with changes through its distinctive capabilities to form a highly robust competitive strategy. This makes a firm's organizational capabilities especially critical facing competitions, because organizational capabilities are the source of competitive advantage (Barney, 1995; Day, 1994, 2011; Grant, 1991, 1996; Teece, Pisano, & Shuen, 1997).

To many organizations worldwide, the evolution of Internet of Things (IoT) is considered as "the next big thing" (Borgia, 2014; Miorandi, Sicari, De Pellegrini, &

Chlamtac, 2012; Weng, 2021; Weng & Lin, 2014; Weng & Lin, 2015) of information technology. The development of various IoT related technologies is expected to affect enterprises' managerial paradigm, including business strategy. IoT attracted attention as a possible source of strategic advantage for firms (Porter & Heppelmann, 2014). It may provide business opportunities for companies, and may even change the future market (Iansiti & Lakhani, 2014). Therefore, aligning with the development of IoT has become critical for the formulation and execution of a firm's business strategy.

The perceived capability of IoT implies that firms make strategic decisions more efficiently. By employing IoT, firms should be able to recognize new business opportunities, identify possible threats, and maintain competitiveness. However, so far studies of the relationship between IoT and business strategy are rare in the literature. To fill this gap, this study intent to investigate the link between IoT and business strategy.

In addition, a firm is a value chain assembled with various value activities (Porter, 1985). These value activities include primary functional operations such as productions, marketing, sales and services, as well as supportive functional operations such as human resource management, research and development (R&D), and information systems. In order to use IoT, a firm needs to integrate IoT with these functional operations. Therefore, these functional operations have influence on the link between IoT and business strategy. Among these functional operations, this research focuses on marketing for several reasons. First, marketing strategy plays a key role in shaping overall business strategy of a firm (Day & Wensley, 1983; Dobni & Luffman, 2003). Second, marketing is tightly related to many other functional operations of a firm, such as production, sales and customer service (Chang, Park, & Chaiy, 2010; Guenzi

& Troilo, 2006; Respício & Captivo, 2008; Rouziès & Hulland, 2014; Tseng, 2016; Wang & Feng, 2012). Finally, IoT enabled products are expected to transform future marketing paradigm (Bulearca & Tamarjan, 2010; Porter & Heppelmann, 2014; Zancul et al., 2016).

Furthermore, in a firm's marketing operations, marketing intelligence is the foundation of overall marketing activities, because marketing decisions rely on the capability of acquiring and interpreting accurate marketing intelligence (Trainor, Krush, & Agnihotri, 2013). Therefore, the objective of this research is to investigate the linkage between IoT and business strategy, and the effect of marketing intelligence in this linkage.

The paper begins with a review of the relevant literature about the relationships between Internet of Things, marketing intelligence and business strategy. Then it proposes a model which links these three variables. Following that, the model is tested using a sample of Taiwanese companies with global operations.

Finally, the findings are presented along with the managerial implications of the study, its limitations and recommendations for future work.

2. Literature Review and Hypotheses Development
2.1 Internet of Things and Business Strategy

Several researchers have elaborated the technological features of Internet of Things (Agarwal & Brem, 2015; Atzori, Iera, & Morabito, 2010; Borgia, 2014; Bradley et al., 2015; Gubbi, Buyya, Marusic, & Palaniswami, 2013; Krotov, 2017; Miorandi et al., 2012; Porter & Heppelmann, 2015). These features are classified and summarized as follows.

1. Ubiquitous sensing: This is the mechanism that the "things" or devices in IoT perceive the surrounding physical environment, detect and record the changes in the environment, and respond to the changes. Ubiquitous sensing is enabled by wireless sensor network (WSN)

technologies (Borgia, 2014; Bradley et al., 2015; Gubbi et al., 2013).

2. Pervasive connectivity: IoT contains multiple layers of communication networking infrastructure to provide the pervasive communications between people and people, people and things, and things and things, to form a smart environment (Atzori et al., 2010; Gubbi et al., 2013).

3. Embedded computing: IoT devices contain embedded hardware and software to work intelligently within the environment. The embedded hardware includes processor chips, data storage units and power units. The embedded software includes embedded operating systems, mobile apps and middleware. In particular, IoT devices can be embedded further in other devices (Gubbi et al., 2013; Krotov, 2017).

4. Real-time analytics: IoT monitored and detected information are invisibly embedded in the environment around users, results in the generation of big data in real-

time which are distributed, stored, processed, presented and interpreted in a seamless, efficient, and easily understandable form (Gubbi et al., 2013; Krotov, 2017).

5. Cloud support: Cloud services are deployed to assist the processing and storage of IoT analytics, and provide IoT users ubiquitous access of supporting services initiated by IoT devices around the smart environment (Atzori et al., 2010; Bradley et al., 2015; Gubbi et al., 2013).

6. Interactive user interface: Visualization, touching and voice are critical for an IoT application as this allows the awareness and interaction of IoT users with the environment. 3D viewing and printing technologies, personal mobile assistants, wearable devices, and augmented-reality devices provide novel interface for users to interact with the smart environment (Bradley et al., 2015; Gubbi et al., 2013).

7. Interconnected smart products: IoT enables evolution of various products such as smart home

appliances, robots, drones, unmanned cars, automated factory machines and business equipment, and many other innovative devices (Krotov, 2017; Miorandi et al., 2012; Porter & Heppelmann, 2015).

8. Cyber-physical convergence: The convergence of computer network, telecom network and IoT triggers further convergence of cyber space and physical space, and results in various smart spaces, such as smart home, smart office, smart factory, smart laboratory, smart store, smart marketplace, smart hospital, smart museum and smart city (Agarwal & Brem, 2015; Bradley et al., 2015; Gubbi et al., 2013; Miorandi et al., 2012).

With these technological features, IoT has been asserted as essential for organizational innovation and adaptation in a changing environment (Lee & Lee, 2015; Y. Li, Hou, Liu, & Liu, 2012), especially for firms with high amounts of connectivity and data (Dlamini et al., 2009; Li et al., 2014a). However, so far few studies have examined the capabilities needed to adopt IoT in an organization, and how these relate to different types of business strategy, particularly from the perspective of an innovative and market-oriented organization. Therefore, to contribute with a required research framework of IoT and business strategy, this study examines the role of IoT capability further in business strategy formation.

IoT capability refers to the firms' ability to integrate firm resources and skills arising from IoT to align with the firms' strategic directions (Bharadwaj, 2000; Grant, 1996). IoT capability enables an organization to exploit and incorporate the above IoT technological features for business value. By using IoT, firms are able to identify new business opportunities and potential threats, and maintain competitiveness, thus establishing the IoT capability to be a source of competitive advantage (Yu, Nguyen, & Chen, 2016). Depending on different industry sectors and business models, a firm with IoT capability could be competent in developing or deploying IoT core components for business applications, or it could be competent in making or using IoT connected products for business benefits, or it could be competent in implementing or operating IoT enabled environments for business value (Porter & Heppelmann, 2014, 2015).

Organizational capabilities play a pivotal role in the business strategy which a firm pursues. The essence of strategy formulation is to design a strategy that makes the most effective use of these core capabilities (Grant, 1991). Furthermore, designing strategy around the most critical capabilities implies that the firm focuses its strategic scope to those activities where it possesses a clear competitive advantage (Teece et al., 1997). These propositions suggest that IoT capability can have potential effect on business strategy formation.

From the strategic management perspective, cost leadership and differentiation are two important approaches to competitive advantage and basic choices of business strategy (Porter, 1980; Porter & Millar, 1985). Furthermore, researchers have argued that cost leadership and differentiation are not mutually exclusive, but rather are compatible approaches to dealing with external situations, and a combination of strategies could lead to success in various circumstances (Hill, 1988; C. B. Li & Li, 2008; Murray, 1988). In the IoT context, whether a firm wants to achieve cost advantage, differentiation advantage, or a combination of both through its IoT capability is an important strategic intent, which causes the firm to formulate and implement IoT facilitated cost leadership strategy, differentiation strategy, or a combination of both types of strategy.

Cost leadership strategy requires organizational capabilities to achieve operational efficiency, including time efficiency, cost efficiency and flexibility. The problem is that people have inadequate time and imperfect accuracy and therefore they are not very good in capturing information about things in the physical world. The IoT sensor technology enables connected devices to sense, observe, and understand the physical world – without the limitations of human-entered data (Haddara & Elragal, 2015). Furthermore, enterprises will be flexible enough to respond to production changes swiftly with IoT capability. The functions of IoT enabled smart factory integrate technologies of many disciplines. IoT capability enables an enterprise to make extensive use of artificial intelligence, simulation, automation, robotics, sensors, data collection systems and networks towards advanced engineering and precision machining. These systems make possible the establishment of efficient, collaborative and sustainable industrial production to achieve cost leadership (Benias & Markopoulos, 2017).

Differentiation strategy requires organizational capabilities to achieve product or service uniqueness for higher customer premium. Products or services differentiation are realized through innovation or customization. IoT capability provides higher accuracy on analyzing and identifying distinctive customer preferences through hidden analytics of interconnected products. Sensor-based information collected through IoT embedded products covers actions of customer purchase and use, and can therefore be analyzed to obtain a much more precise and complete picture of the customer's characteristics and of their preferences (Ng, Scharf, Pogrebna, & Maull, 2015). Smart laboratories can provide test fields for innovative products and services before delivery to customers. Customer feedbacks are collected and transmitted in real-time through various sensor networks and supportive cloud services for further refinement of innovation or customization. Thus IoT capability could expand opportunities for product or service differentiation, moving competition away from cost alone.

Therefore, the following two hypotheses are proposed:

H1a. IoT capability is positively associated with cost leadership strategy formation.

H1b. IoT capability is positively associated with differentiation strategy formation.

2.2 Internet of Things and Marketing Intelligence

Effective marketing requires adequate information for planning and allocating resources properly to different markets, products, territories, and marketing tools (Kotler, 1977). Marketing intelligence is the systematically collected and extracted information for making marketing decisions. Marketing intelligence is a critical component for overall marketing activities of a firm. Acquisition and effective use of marketing intelligence is vital in shaping the firm's sustainable competitive advantage (Jaworski & Kohli, 1993; Kohli & Jaworski, 1990). Marketing intelligence capability concerns a firm's ability to learn about customers, competitors, channel members and the broader market environment in which it operates (Day, 1994; Morgan, Slotegraaf, & Vorhies, 2009).

IoT capability is expected to enhance marketing intelligence capability, because IoT capability enables a firm with better ability to sense and collect information from customers and competitors (Yu et al., 2016). IoT capability indicates the ability in merging of the digital world with the world of things. It involves the ability of convergence of the industrial systems with the power of advanced computing, analytics, low-cost sensing, and new levels of connectivity provided by the internet (Agarwal & Brem, 2015). For a firm with IoT capability, large scale real-time customer surveys can be conducted with the assistance of sensing and recognition technology. Augmented reality enhanced user interface allows users to view and test products and services using their smartphones, tablets or 3D viewing glasses. The big data from IoT connected products provides a clear picture of product use, showing the features customers prefer. By comparing usage patterns, firms can identify finer market segmentation information (Porter & Heppelmann, 2015).

Firms can then apply this knowledge to generate more valuable intelligence, and develop more sophisticated pricing strategies that better match price and value at the market segment.

Furthermore, it is easier in a smart environment such as a smart marketplace or a smart store to collect and disseminate user opinions and user experiences about competitors' products or services (Gubbi et al., 2013). The ubiquitous sensing with intelligent pattern recognition and machine learning functionalities enables the analysis and simulation of competitors' products and services. Using this information, further realization of competitors' products or services can be accomplished digitally or physically in a smart laboratory using 3D animation or 3D printing technology. The big data of feedback opinions collected from customers and distributors can also be exploited to make more accurate analysis of competitors' situations. IoT embedded analytics can invoke corrective processes to address immediate operational issues or inform managers of discoveries regarding competitors' strategic moves that will impact their short-term and long-term business activities (Lee & Lee, 2015).

IoT capability also facilitates the collaborations between firms and business partners. Information sharing and collaboration in the IoT can occur between people, between people and things, and between things. Firms with IoT capability are easier to form virtual alliances or virtual groups with partners. These partners could be customers, suppliers, intermediaries, governments and competitors, all of which are important in IoT context (Yu et al., 2016). Sensing a predefined event is usually the first step for information sharing and collaboration. Information sharing and collaboration enhance situational awareness and avoid information delay and distortion (Lee & Lee, 2015). This is the essence of marketing intelligence.

As such, IoT capability can enhance firm's marketing intelligence acquisition efforts, representing the extent to which they can generate and disseminate marketing intelligence, and which may lead to novel interpretations and recombination of prompt responses to marketing situations. Thus with IoT capability, a firm is able to transform marketing intelligence capability and enhance marketing results. In summary, we propose the following hypotheses:

H2. IoT capability is positively associated with marketing intelligence capability.

2.3 Marketing Intelligence and Business Strategy

Marketing intelligence is about staying ahead of the competition by gathering information which could be converted to actionable intelligence and which can then be applied to both short and long term strategic planning (Ettorre, 1995; Slater & Narver, 2000). Marketing intelligence is considered as a strategic resource that enables a firm to strengthen its opportunity recognition, threat identification and achieve a positional advantage over its competitors (Day, 1994). Hence it is related to the firm's business strategy formation.

Business strategy formation is comprised of mission and goal clarity, situation analysis, comprehensiveness of alternative evaluation, and strategy formation process (Slater, Olson, & Hult, 2006). A business strategy concerns the competitive positioning, market segmentation and industry environment of a company (Porter, 1980). To survive, grow and sustain, a firm needs to constantly monitor its internal and external status for possible changes. Thus the formulation and execution of a business strategy rely heavily on the collection, extraction, analyze, interpretation and prediction on internal and external status data of the company, in order to make accurate managerial decisions (Claver-Cortés, Pertusa-Ortega, & Molina-Azorín, 2012; McAfee & Brynjolfsson, 2012). Therefore, a firm's marketing intelligence capability is critical in facilitating its business strategy formation. Furthermore, business strategies of most companies are frequently a combination of their intended strategies and the emergent strategies (Mintzberg, 1985). Business leaders need to analyze the status information of emergence and to make strategy adjustment when appropriate (Mintzberg & Waters, 1985). For this purpose, marketing intelligence capability is also essential as the ability for the strategic decisions to be accurately updated and aligned with competition changes (Akter, Wamba, Gunasekaran, Dubey, & Childe, 2016; Janssen, van der Voort, & Wahyudi, 2017).

Marketing intelligence capability enables a firm to acquire and analyze the cost structures and distinctive features of products and services of peers in the marketplace. It helps the firm to determine which market segments are suitable for cost leadership, and which market segments are feasible for differentiation.

Marketing intelligence about cost analytics of all levels needs to be collected and accurately analyzed for a firm to maintain a viable leading cost status. Marketing intelligence about customer preferences and distinctive features are required for a firm to determine the need to differentiate its products against the need to keep its cost structure under control in order to offer a distinctive product at a competitive price (Slater et al., 2006; Xie, Wu, Xiao, & Hu, 2016).

Therefore, the following two hypotheses are proposed:

H3a. Marketing intelligence capability is positively associated with cost leadership strategy formation.

H3b. Marketing intelligence capability is positively associated with differentiation strategy formation.

Based on our proposed hypotheses, the research framework is illustrated in Figure 1.

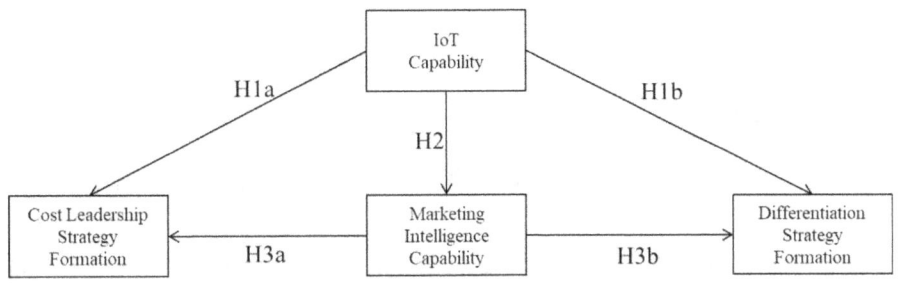

Figure 1   Research framework

3. Research Method

3.1 Survey Instrument

The survey instrument was developed using questions derived from the literature on information technology capabilities, marketing capabilities, and Porter's typology of competitive strategies discussed previously. We operationalized the study variables by using multi-item reflective measures on a 7-point scale (Jarvis, MacKenzie, & Podsakoff, 2003).

Following the definition of information technology capability by Bharadwaj (2000), a firm's IoT capability is measured here by its ability to develop or deploy IoT based resources, which include the tangible IoT resources, the intangible IoT resources, and the human IoT resources. The tangible IoT resources are physical things such as IoT components, IoT connected products, and IoT enabled smart environments. The intangible IoT resources are assets such as knowledge, know-how, and synergy about IoT. The human IoT resources comprise technical and managerial IoT staffs. Thus we measure the core capability arising from IoT with three items according to the utilization of the three types of IoT based resources.

A firm's marketing intelligence capability concerns its competency in intelligence generation, intelligence dissemination, and responsiveness (Kohli & Jaworski, 1990; Kohli, Jaworski, & Kumar, 1993). Marketing intelligence capability is operationalized as the accessibility and utilization of resources and activities within a firm to collect and analyze market information, and utilize it to develop effective marketing programs.

The ability to effectively gather and disseminate customer and competitor information is critical for marketing intelligence capability (Kohli et al., 1993; Narver & Slater, 1990). This four-item scale was adapted from Vorhies, Morgan, and Autry (2009) and Trainor et al. (2013).

The construct of cost leadership strategy formation was measured using four items that reflect the extent to which a firm forms a cost-oriented strategy. The formation of cost leadership strategy aims at achieving low manufacturing and distribution costs (Dess & Davis, 1984; Narver & Slater, 1990; Porter, 1980). The third item was the economic scale. A firm can usually lower cost through economies of scale or superior manufacturing processes (Porter, 1980, 1985). Finally, formation of cost leadership is often reflected in lower price of products or services (Dess & Davis, 1984; Robinson & Pearce, 1988).

The construct of differentiation strategy formation was measured using four items that reflect the extent to which a firm forms a differentiation strategy. Differentiation implies being unique or distinct from competitors by providing superior functionality or customized feature within products or services to customers (Porter, 1980; Wu, 2004). Extending Porter's business strategy framework, Miller (1988) discriminated differentiation strategy based on innovation from that based on intensive marketing (Miller, 1986, 1988). This distinction forms two items included in the construct.

All items for this study were assessed with a 7-point Likert scale ranging from "strongly disagree" to "strongly agree." Furthermore, firm size, IT department size and industry sector were used as control variables, as these variables have been noted in several studies to affect deployment of information technologies (Liu, Ke, Wei, Gu, & Chen, 2010; Teo, Wei, & Benbasat, 2003).

Table 1 presents the items used to measure each of the independent and dependent construct variables.

Table 1 Constructs and items used in the survey

	Construct and item description (1 – strongly disagree; 7 – strongly agree)
IoT:	Internet of Things capability
IoT1:	My company is competent in developing or deploying IoT technologies such as IoT components, IoT connected products or IoT enabled environments.
IoT2:	We possess sophisticated IoT knowledge, intelligence and synergy.
IoT3:	Our employees are proficient in IoT technologies and related managerial topics.
MIC:	Marketing intelligence capability
MIC1:	My company is competent in collecting information about customers and competitors
MIC2:	We are proficient in tracking customer needs and wants
MIC3:	We are skillful in analyzing and disseminating marketing information
MIC4:	We are competent in developing effective marketing programs
CLS:	Cost leadership strategy formation
CLS1:	We provide low cost products or services based on manufacturing efficiency
CLS2:	Our products or services have lower distribution cost than our competitors
CLS3:	We develop and deliver products or services with economy of scale
CLS4:	Our products or services have lower prices than competitors in the market
DFS:	Differentiation strategy formation
DFS1:	We deliver products or services with superior functionality to our competitors
DFS2:	We provide products or services with customized feature to our customers
DFS3:	Our firm differentiates our products or services based on innovation
DFS4:	Our firm differentiates our products or services based on intensive marketing
Control Variables (rescaled)	
Industry:	Industry sectors of firms. 1 for service firms and 0 for manufacturing firms.
Firm Size:	Total number of employees.
IT Size:	Total numbers of IT staffs.

3.2 Sample and Data Collection

Enterprises operating in Taiwan were surveyed in order to test the hypotheses. A questionnaire designed in accordance with Table 1 above was implemented as the survey instrument. It was then pretested with 13 executives and managers. The pretesting focused on instrument clarity, question wording, and validity. Members of the testing sample were invited to comment on the questions and wording of the questionnaire. The comments of these respondents then provided a basis for revisions to the questionnaire to establish content validity.

A sample of 1,000 firms was randomly selected from the top 5,000 list of the largest companies in Taiwan published by a credit information service firm. Most of the companies in the list are public listed corporations with international operations. The survey, which took three months to complete, was initially conducted by postal mail and e-mail, and then followed up with telephone calls and in-person visits. A total of 217 responses were received, of which 15 were unusable and eliminated. The remaining 202 responses were used in this study, for a response rate of 20.2%.

The mean differences between responding and non-responding firms were compared along firm attributes using t-tests and all statistics were non-significant ($p > 0.5$). Furthermore, the responses were classified into two groups to examine whether there was any response bias. The responses received during the first two months were classified as early returns, and those received during the last months as late returns. The two groups were then compared for any significant difference in responses using the chi-square test of independence. No significant difference was found between the two groups, supporting that response bias is not an issue in this study (Armstron & Overton, 1977). Table 2 shows the profile of the final sample list.

Table 2 Profile of the final sampling firms

	Sample size	Percentage
Industry		
Manufacturing	92	45.5%
Services	110	54.5%
Total	202	100.0%
Firm size		
Under 100	50	24.8%
100-199	53	26.2%
200-499	40	19.8%
500 and above	59	29.2%
Total	202	100.0%
IT department size		
Under 5	67	33.2%
5-19	62	30.7%
20 and above	73	36.1%
Total	202	100.0%

4. Results

Our goal was to investigate the impact of a firm's IoT capability on marketing intelligence capability and business strategy formation, and the possible mediation role of marketing intelligence capability. The empirical results were expected to demonstrate that a firm's formation of business strategy, such as cost leadership strategy and differentiation strategy, is influenced by IoT capability and marketing intelligence capability. The results were also expected to verify the mediating role of marketing intelligence capability in the link between IoT capability and business strategy formation. Finally, the results were used to test the relationship between IoT capability and marketing intelligence capability.

4.1 Reliability and Validity

The reliability of the survey instrument was tested by using Cronbach's alpha (Cronbach, 1951) to assess the internal consistency of the proposed constructs listed in Table 1. Cronbach's alpha tests the interrelationship among the items composing a construct to determine if the items measure a single construct. Nunnally and Bernstein (1994) recommended a threshold alpha value of .7. Cicchetti et al. (2011) further suggested the following reliability guidelines for determining significance: $\alpha < .70$ (unacceptable), $.70 \leq \alpha < .80$ (fair), $.80 \leq \alpha < .90$ (good), and $\alpha > .90$ (excellent).

Content validity (Straub, 1989) refers to the extent to which the instrument measures what it is designed to measure. Most of our measures used in the study were adopted from relevant studies. Although basing the study on the established literature provided a considerable level of validity, the study's validity was further improved by pre-testing the instrument on a panel of experts comprising 13 business executives and managers.

Table 3 summarizes the descriptive statistics and results of the reliability and validity tests. The reliability of the instrument was examined using composite reliability estimates by employing Cronbach's α. All the coefficients exceeded Nunnally's recommended level (0.70) of internal consistency (Cicchetti et al., 2011; Nunnally & Bernstein, 1994). In addition, factor analysis was performed to confirm the construct validity. The results supported the constructs of our research model. The discriminant validity was confirmed since items for each constructs loaded on to single factors with all loadings greater than 0.8. These results confirmed that each of the construct in our hypothesized model is unidimensional and factorially distinct, and that all items used to operationalize a construct is loaded onto a single factor.

Table 3 Descriptive statistics and reliability and validity test

Construct	Item	Mean	SD	Cronbach's alpha	Cronbach's alpha if item deleted	Factor loading on single factor
IoT	IoT1	4.123	1.554	0.815	0.752	0.851
	IoT2	3.671	1.479		0.731	0.864
	IoT3	4.708	1.554		0.756	0.849
MIC	MIC1	4.755	1.022	0.920	0.922	0.854
	MIC2	4.787	.931		0.886	0.923
	MIC3	4.828	.931		0.901	0.890
	MIC4	4.764	.857		0.878	0.940
CLS	CLS1	4.329	.910	0.951	0.933	0.931
	CLS2	4.375	.863		0.937	0.941
	CLS3	3.988	.729		0.943	0.937

	CLS4	4.724	.990		0.930	0.946
DFS	DFS1	4.675	.962	0.891	0.837	0.911
	DFS2	4.616	1.106		0.859	0.872
	DFS3	4.616	1.039		0.870	0.848
	DFS4	4.787	.959		0.873	0.848

Table 4 presents the results of a factor analysis. A four-factor structure emerged with all predefined indicators loading on to their respective constructs, which thereby affirmed convergent validity and unidimensionality of the constructs. The model explained 80.665% of the variance.

Table 4　Factor analysis

Construct	Item	Factor1	Factor2	Factor3	Factor4
IoT	IoT1	**.842**	.112	.133	.047
	IoT2	**.817**	.086	.130	.246
	IoT3	**.838**	.042	.084	.106
MIC	MIC1	.121	**.781**	.225	.231
	MIC2	.053	**.902**	.157	.180
	MIC3	.051	**.812**	.250	.245
	MIC4	.122	**.853**	.239	.294
CLS	CLS1	.099	.166	**.908**	.189

	CLS2	.168	.306	**.820**	.281
	CLS3	.184	.293	**.819**	.268
	CLS4	.092	.186	**.911**	.214
DFS	DFS1	.139	.252	.257	**.819**
	DFS2	.163	.228	.153	**.831**
	DFS3	.169	.249	.196	**.775**
	DFS4	.064	.249	.386	**.711**

Table 5 summarizes the correlations among different factors. We also assessed discriminant validity on the basis of the construct correlation that Campbell and Fiske (1959) proposed. The tests indicated acceptable results with respect to discriminant validity.

Table 5　Construct correlation

Construct	1	2	3	4	5	6	7
1. IoT	1						
2. MIC	0.254**	1					
3. CLS	0.322**	0.532**	1				
4. DFS	0.355**	0.580**	0.576**	1			
5. Industry	0.131	-0.062	0.080	0.046	1		
6. Firm Size	0.150	0.006	0.099	0.055	-0.100	1	
7. IT Size	0.148	0.068	0.148	0.138	-2.790**	0.402**	1

*$p < 0.05$, **$p < 0.01$

4.2 Tests of Hypotheses

To test our hypotheses, multiple regression analysis was performed using SPSS version 21. We examined the degree to which our data met appropriate statistical assumptions in the case of multiple regression analysis such as normality and linearity, and our data met the requisite assumptions.

Table 6 summarizes the test results regarding the parameter estimates and p-values of the hypothesized model in Figure 1. We also included industry, firm size and IT department size as control variables in the analysis.

Table 6 Tests results of the hypothesized model

DV	Explanatory variable				Control variable						R^2
	IoT		MIC		Industry		Firm Size		IT Size		
	Est	p	Est	p	Est	p	Est	p	Est	p	
MIC	0.271	0.000***			-0.097	0.184	-0.054	0.476	0.023	0.774	0.076
CLS	0.291	0.000***			0.077	0.278	0.014	0.847	0.120	0.118	0.119
DFS	0.340	0.000***			0.028	0.687	-0.038	0.600	0.111	0.146	0.135
CLS			0.533	0.000***	0.156	0.012	0.058	0.365	0.131	0.050	0.321
DFS			0.579	0.000***	0.119	0.051	0.012	0.845	0.127	0.052	0.360
CLS	0.158	0.012*	0.492	0.000***	0.125	0.052	0.041	0.524	0.109	0.102	0.343
DFS	0.197	0.001**	0.529	0.000***	0.080	0.181	-0.010	0.873	0.099	0.122	0.393

DV: Dependent variable;   Est: Estimate;   p: P-value
*p < 0.05, **p < 0.01, ***p < 0.001

The results in Table 6 supported our hypotheses. The direct effects of IoT on CLS and DFS, IoT on MIC, and MIC on CLS and DFS are tested significant. In the links of IoT on CLS of hypothesis H1a and IoT on DFS of hypothesis H1b, in addition to the found direct effects, partial mediation effects of MIC in the links were also found. This indicates that IoT capability influences business strategy formation with a direct effect and through a mediation effect. The test procedure concerning mediation follows the suggestion of Baron and Kenny (1986). We compared the proposed mediation model with an alternative direct effect model without MIC variable. The mediation model explains more variance on CLS ($R^2 = 0.343$) and DFS ($R^2 = 0.393$) than the direct effect model ($R^2 = 0.119$ and $R^2 = 0.135$). The test results show that positive relationships exist between IoT and MIC ($\beta= 0.271$, $p < 0.001$), between MIC and CLS ($\beta= 0.533$, $p < 0.001$), and between MIC and DFS ($\beta= 0.579$, $p < 0.001$). Furthermore, the significant relationships between IoT and CLS ($\beta= 0.291$, $p < 0.001$) and between IoT and DFS ($\beta= 0.340$, $p < 0.001$) in the direct effect model is greater than those in the mediation model ($\beta= 0.158$, $p < 0.05$ and $\beta= 0.197$, $p < 0.01$). Taking into account these results as a whole, we thus conclude that the effect of IoT capability on business strategy formation is partially mediated by marketing intelligence capability (Baron & Kenny, 1986). The effects of paths in Figure 1 are summarized in Table 7.

Table 7 Effects of paths in the hypothesized model

Hypothesis	path	Effect from test results
H1a	IoT → CLS	Direct effect supported Partial mediation of MIC supported
H1b	IoT → DFS	Direct effect supported Partial mediation of MIC supported
H2	IoT → MIC	Direct effect supported
H3a	MIC → CLS	Direct effect supported
H3b	MIC → DFS	Direct effect supported

5. Discussion and Conclusions

5.1 Research Implications

This study investigated the impact of a firm's IoT capability on business strategy formation, and tested the possible mediating role of marketing intelligence capability. By supporting the research hypotheses, this study could be directed toward helping managers and practitioners realize the links between organizational capabilities and business strategy formation.

First, the cultivation of organizational capabilities, in general, is expected to enhance an organization's business strategies and further elevate its competitive advantage (Day, 1994; Grant, 1991; Ravichandran & Lertwongsatien, 2005). This study substantiates the positive correlation between a firm's organizational capabilities and business strategy formation. In particular, our results support the positive correlations between two different organizational capabilities and the formation of two types of business strategies. The findings demonstrate that both IoT capability and marketing intelligence capability have positive effects on the formation of both cost leadership strategy and differentiation strategy, which could further lead to competitive advantage (Porter, 1980, 1985). Therefore, the study serves to inform business managers that firms should do more than just invest in innovative technologies or marketing operations. They need to identify and build distinctive capabilities and put them in productive use. This study suggests that both IoT capability and marketing intelligence capability are worthy of attention in this regards. The findings that these capabilities may impact business strategy formation indicate that their influence on a firm are cross-functional and may transcend managerial hierarchy.

Second, this study identifies a mediator in the association between IoT and business strategy. While IoT capability is shown to positively influence business strategy formation, our findings also point out that the link between IoT capability and business strategy formation is partially mediated by marketing intelligence capability. Our study is unique that it explores the link between IoT capability and marketing intelligence capability, and reveals the mediating role of marketing intelligence capability on the relationship between IoT capability and business strategy formation. For the partial mediation to be established, both of the links between IoT capability and marketing intelligence capability and between marketing intelligence capability and business strategy formation need to be significant, and the influence of IoT capability on business strategy formation is alleviated with the presence of marketing intelligence capability (Baron & Kenny, 1986). That is, in addition to the direct effect of IoT capability on business strategy formation, there is also an indirect effect through marketing intelligence capability. These two effects contribute to the total effect of IoT capability on business strategy formation. From the literature contribution perspective, few of the extant literature refer to what happens to the inside of a firm when IoT is introduced. Furthermore, most of the present research draws more attention to the analysis of how IoT could influence business performance than to the discussion of how IoT and marketing function together on business strategy through the mediating role of marketing intelligence. Our findings support not only the marketing orientation concept of Jaworski and Kohli (1993), but also the hierarchy model of capabilities of Grant (1996). From the managerial implication perspective, the marketing department in a firm is skillful at sensing and understanding the outside environment. If a business strategy of a firm can fit into its surroundings, its performance is usually enhanced. Thus, a marketing department in a firm becomes critical for a firm to make its business strategies fit with its surroundings. Our findings suggest that IoT capability can facilitate the marketing department of a firm for the generation, dissemination and analysis of marketing intelligence, so as to help shaping the firm's business strategy for competitive advantage.

Finally, our findings indicate the similar effects of organizational capabilities on the two types of business strategies. Both cost leadership strategy formation and differentiation strategy formation are positively influenced by IoT capability and marketing intelligence capability. This demonstrates that IoT capability and marketing intelligence capability are both enabling capabilities for business strategy formation, regardless of the strategy typology. In essence, IoT capability and its output, pervasive sensing and connectivity with embedded analytics, enable firms to deploy and operate in smart environments, and thus could enhance the functional level operations with efficiency and flexibility to achieve cost leadership or differentiation, or a combination of both. In addition, it is also because of the cross-functional nature of pervasive sensing and connectivity with embedded analytics, IoT capability can have a positive influence on some other organizational capabilities, such as marketing intelligence capability. Marketing intelligence capability and its output, marketing intelligence, enable firms to anticipate and understand better the customer needs and the competitive situation, to process this information faster and to develop products and services with lower cost or with differentiated features, which empower firms to sustain a competitive advantage. Furthermore, IoT capability and marketing intelligence capability may facilitate firms to identify opportunities for improvement and novel solutions. One of the opportunities is to explore the feasibility of mass customization, which may achieve cost leadership and differentiation simultaneously (Kotha, 1995; Pine, Victor, & Boynton, 1993).

5.2 Study Limitations and Further Research

Although this study reported meaningful implications regarding the development of multidimensional measures of constructs in our hypothesized framework, it should be realized that the validity of an instrument cannot be firmly established on the basis of a single study. In this study, all data used for tests were collected from firms based in Taiwan. Taiwan is a relatively efficient and competitive arena for adopting IoT technologies, but it has its own industry characteristics. In particular, manufacturing and retail industries are the dominant industries in Taiwan. Therefore, practitioners and academics are suggested to interpret our findings as a reference model rather than generalizing our measures to different research context.

Further research efforts which focus on accumulating more empirical evidence for assessing and validating empirical data are recommended to overcome the limitations of the present study. Such research is required to address how other emerging technologies relate to business strategies and functional operations. For example, wearable interface technology (Chan, Esteve, Fourniols, Escriba, & Campo, 2012; Chen, Wang, Huang, Wei, & Wang, 2015; Gruebler, Berenz, & Suzuki, 2012) and augmented reality technology (Chung, Han, & Joun, 2015; Meža, Turk, & Dolenc, 2015; Petersen & Stricker, 2015) have received inadequate attention from strategic considerations and organizational capability theories. Further research could also investigate the relative importance of the factors affecting each stage of the strategy shaping process. These efforts should involve studies identifying the organizational capabilities which affect business operation, information processing, and decision support. In addition, special attention could be focused on data collected in various sub-industries or specific contexts over an extended period of time. The analysis of these data may enable conclusions to be drawn about more generalized relationships among business level strategy, functional level strategy, and technology based organizational capability.

References

Agarwal, N., & Brem, A. (2015). Strategic business transformation through technology convergence: implications from General Electrics industrial internet initiative. *International Journal of Technology Management, 67*(2/3/4), 196-214.

Akter, S., Wamba, S. F., Gunasekaran, A., Dubey, R., &

Childe, S. J. (2016). How to improve firm performance using big data analytics capability and business strategy alignment? *International Journal of Production Economics, 182*, 113-131. doi:10.1016/j.ijpe.2016.08.018

Armstron, J. S., & Overton, T. S. (1977). Estimating Nonresponse Bias in Mail Surveys. *JMR, Journal of Marketing Research (pre-1986), 14*(3), 396.

Atzori, L., Iera, A., & Morabito, G. (2010). The Internet of Things: A survey. *Computer Networks, 54*(15), 2787-2805. doi:10.1016/j.comnet.2010.05.010

Barney, J. B. (1995). Looking inside for competitive advantage. *The Academy of Management Executive, 9*(4), 49-61.

Baron, R. M., & Kenny, D. A. (1986). The moderator–mediator variable distinction in social psychological research: Conceptual, strategic, and statistical considerations. *Journal of Personality and Social Psychology, 51*(6), 1173-1182. doi:10.1037/0022-

3514.51.6.1173

Benias, N., & Markopoulos, A. P. (2017). *A review on the readiness level and cyber-security challenges in Industry 4.0.* Paper presented at the Design Automation, Computer Engineering, Computer Networks and Social Media Conference (SEEDA-CECNSM), 2017 South Eastern European.

Bharadwaj, A. S. (2000). A resource-based perspective on information technology capability and firm performance: an empirical investigation. *MIS Quarterly, 24*(1), 169-196.

Borgia, E. (2014). The Internet of Things vision: Key features, applications and open issues. *Computer Communications, 54,* 1-31. doi:10.1016/j.comcom.2014.09.008

Bradley, D., Russell, D., Ferguson, I., Isaacs, J., MacLeod, A., & White, R. (2015). The Internet of Things – The future or the end of mechatronics. *Mechatronics, 27,* 57-74.

doi:10.1016/j.mechatronics.2015.02.005

Bulearca, M., & Tamarjan, D. (2010). Augmented Reality: A Sustainable Marketing Tool? *Global Business and Management Research, 2*(2/3), 237-252.

Campbell, D., T., & Fiske, D., W. (1959). Convergent and discriminant validation by the multitrait-multimethod matrix. *Psychological Bulletin, 56*(2), 81-105.

Chan, M., Esteve, D., Fourniols, J. Y., Escriba, C., & Campo, E. (2012). Smart wearable systems: current status and future challenges. *Artif Intell Med, 56*(3), 137-156. doi:10.1016/j.artmed.2012.09.003

Chang, W., Park, J. E., & Chaiy, S. (2010). How does CRM technology transform into organizational performance? A mediating role of marketing capability. *Journal of Business Research, 63*(8), 849-855.

doi:https://doi.org/10.1016/j.jbusres.2009.07.003

Chen, B., Wang, X., Huang, Y., Wei, K., & Wang, Q. (2015). A foot-wearable interface for locomotion mode recognition based on discrete contact force distribution. *Mechatronics, 32*, 12-21. doi:10.1016/j.mechatronics.2015.09.002

Chung, N., Han, H., & Joun, Y. (2015). Tourists' intention to visit a destination: The role of augmented reality (AR) application for a heritage site. *Computers in Human Behavior, 50*, 588-599. doi:10.1016/j.chb.2015.02.068

Cicchetti, D. V., Koenig, K., Klin, A., Volkmar, F. R., Paul, R., & Sparrow, S. (2011). From Bayes through marginal utility to effect sizes: a guide to understanding the clinical and statistical significance of the results of autism research findings. *J Autism Dev Disord, 41*(2), 168-174. doi:10.1007/s10803-010-1035-6

Claver-Cortés, E., Pertusa-Ortega, E. M., & Molina-Azorín, J. F. (2012). Characteristics of organizational structure relating to hybrid competitive strategy: Implications for performance. *Journal of Business Research, 65*(7), 993-1002. doi:10.1016/j.jbusres.2011.04.012

Cronbach, L. (1951). Coefficient alpha and the internal structure of tests. *Psychometrika, 16*(3), 297-334. doi:10.1007/BF02310555

Day, G. S. (1994). The Capabilities of Market-Driven Organizations. *Journal of Marketing, 58*(4), 37-52. doi:10.2307/1251915

Day, G. S. (2011). Closing the Marketing Capabilities Gap. *Journal of Marketing, 75*(4), 183-195. Retrieved from <Go to ISI>://WOS:000292065800016

Day, G. S., & Wensley, R. (1983). Marketing Theory with a Strategic Orientation. *Journal of Marketing, 47*(4), 79-89. doi:10.2307/1251401

Dess, G. G., & Davis, P. S. (1984). Porter's (1980) Generic Strategies as Determinants of Strategic

Group Membership and Organizational Performance. *Academy of Management Journal, 27*(3), 467-488. doi:10.2307/256040

Dobni, C. B., & Luffman, G. (2003). Determining the scope and impact of market orientation profiles on strategy implementation and performance. *Strategic Management Journal, 24*(6), 577-585.

Ettorre, B. (1995). Managing competitive intelligence. *Management Review, 84*(10), 15.

Grant, R. M. (1991). The Resource-Based Theory of Competitive Advantage: Implications for Strategy Formulation. *California Management Review, 33*(3), 114-135. Retrieved from http://search.ebscohost.com/login.aspx?direct=true&db=bth&AN=4761020&lang=zh-tw&site=ehost-live

Grant, R. M. (1996). Prospering in Dynamically-Competitive Environments: Organizational Capability as Knowledge Integration. *Organization*

Science, 7(4), 375-387. Retrieved from http://www.jstor.org/stable/2635098

Gruebler, A., Berenz, V., & Suzuki, K. (2012). Emotionally Assisted Human–Robot Interaction Using a Wearable Device for Reading Facial Expressions. *Advanced Robotics, 26*(10), 1143-1159. doi:10.1080/01691864.2012.686349

Gubbi, J., Buyya, R., Marusic, S., & Palaniswami, M. (2013). Internet of Things (IoT): A vision, architectural elements, and future directions. *Future Generation Computer Systems, 29*(7), 1645-1660. doi:10.1016/j.future.2013.01.010

Guenzi, P., & Troilo, G. (2006). Developing marketing capabilities for customer value creation through Marketing–Sales integration. *Industrial Marketing Management, 35*(8), 974-988. doi:https://doi.org/10.1016/j.indmarman.2006.06.006

Haddara, M., & Elragal, A. (2015). The Readiness of

ERP Systems for the Factory of the Future. *Procedia Computer Science, 64,* 721-728.

Hill, C. V. L. (1988). Difierentiation versus low cost or differentiation and low cost: A contingency framework. *Academy of Management Review, 13*(3), 401-412.

Iansiti, M., & Lakhani, K. R. (2014). Digital Ubiquity - How Connections, Sensors, and Data Are Revolutionizing Business. *Harvard Business Review, November,* 91-99.

Janssen, M., van der Voort, H., & Wahyudi, A. (2017). Factors influencing big data decision-making quality. *Journal of Business Research, 70,* 338-345. doi:10.1016/j.jbusres.2016.08.007

Jarvis, C. B., MacKenzie, S. B., & Podsakoff, P. M. (2003). A critical review of construct indicators and measurement model misspecification in marketing and consumer research. *Journal of consumer research, 30*(2), 199-218.

Jaworski, B. J., & Kohli, A. K. (1993). Market Orientation: Antecedents and Consequences. *Journal of Marketing, 57*(3), 53-70. doi:10.2307/1251854

Kohli, A. K., & Jaworski, B. J. (1990). Market Orientation: The Construct, Research Propositions, and Managerial Implications. *Journal of Marketing, 54*(2), 1-18. doi:10.2307/1251866

Kohli, A. K., Jaworski, B. J., & Kumar, A. (1993). MARKOR: A Measure of Market Orientation. *Journal of Marketing Research, 30*(4), 467-477. doi:10.2307/3172691

Kotha, S. (1995). Mass Customization: Implementing the Emerging Paradigm for Competitive Advantage. *Strategic Management Journal, 16*, 21-42. Retrieved from http://www.jstor.org/stable/2486768

Kotler, P. (1977). From sales obsession to marketing effectiveness. *Harvard Business Review, November-December*, 67-75.

Krotov, V. (2017). The Internet of Things and new business opportunities. *Business Horizons, 60*(6), 831-841. doi:https://doi.org/10.1016/j.bushor.2017.07.009

Lee, I., & Lee, K. (2015). The Internet of Things (IoT): Applications, investments, and challenges for enterprises. *Business Horizons, 58*(4), 431-440. doi:10.1016/j.bushor.2015.03.008

Li, C. B., & Li, J. J. L. (2008). Achieving superior financial performance in China: Differentiation, cost Leadership, or both? *Journal of International Marketing, 16*(3), 1-22.

Li, Y., Hou, M., Liu, H., & Liu, Y. (2012). Towards a theoretical framework of strategic decision, supporting capability and information sharing under the context of Internet of Things. *Information Technology and Management, 13*(4), 205-216. doi:10.1007/s10799-012-0121-1

Liu, H., Ke, W., Wei, K. K., Gu, J., & Chen, H. (2010).

The role of institutional pressures and organizational culture in the firm's intention to adopt internet-enabled supply chain management systems. *Journal of Operations Management, 28*(5), 372-384. doi:10.1016/j.jom.2009.11.010

McAfee, A., & Brynjolfsson, E. (2012). Big data - The management revolution. *Harvard Business Review, 90*(10), 60-68.

Meža, S., Turk, Ž., & Dolenc, M. (2015). Measuring the potential of augmented reality in civil engineering. *Advances in Engineering Software, 90*, 1-10. doi:10.1016/j.advengsoft.2015.06.005

Miller, D. (1986). Configurations of Strategy and Structure: Towards a Synthesis. *Strategic Management Journal, 7*(3), 233-249. Retrieved from http://www.jstor.org/stable/2486075

Miller, D. (1988). Relating porter's business strategies to environment and structure: analysis and performance implications. *Academy of Management*

Journal, 31(2), 280-308.

Mintzberg, H. (1985). Strategy formation in an adhocracy. *Administrative Science Quarterly 30*(2), 160-197.

Mintzberg, H., & Waters, J. A. (1985). Of strategies, deliberate and emergent. *Strategic Management Journal, 6*(3), 257-272.

Miorandi, D., Sicari, S., De Pellegrini, F., & Chlamtac, I. (2012). Internet of things: Vision, applications and research challenges. *Ad Hoc Networks, 10*(7), 1497-1516. doi:10.1016/j.adhoc.2012.02.016

Morgan, N. A., Slotegraaf, R. J., & Vorhies, D. W. (2009). Linking marketing capabilities with profit growth. *International Journal of Research in Marketing, 26*(4), 284-293.

Murray, A. I. (1988). A contingency view of Porter's "generic strategies". *Academy of Management Review, 13*(3), 390-400.

Narver, J. C., & Slater, S. F. (1990). The Effect of a

Market Orientation on Business Profitability. *Journal of Marketing, 54*(4), 20-35. doi:10.2307/1251757

Ng, I., Scharf, K., Pogrebna, G., & Maull, R. (2015). Contextual variety, Internet-of-Things and the choice of tailoring over platform: Mass customisation strategy in supply chain management. *International Journal of Production Economics, 159*, 76-87. doi:10.1016/j.ijpe.2014.09.007

Nunnally, J. C., & Bernstein, I. H. (1994). *Psychometric theory* (3 ed.). New York: McGraw-Hill.

Petersen, N., & Stricker, D. (2015). Cognitive Augmented Reality. *Computers & Graphics, 53*, 82-91. doi:10.1016/j.cag.2015.08.009

Pine, B. J., Victor, B., & Boynton, A. C. (1993). Making mass customization work. *Harvard Business Review, 71*(5), 108-111.

Porter, M. E. (1980). *Competitive strategy*. New York: Free Press.

Porter, M. E. (1985). *Competitive advantage.* New York: Free Press.

Porter, M. E., & Heppelmann, J. E. (2014). How smart, connected products are transforming competition. *Harvard Business Review, 92*(11), 64-88.

Porter, M. E., & Heppelmann, J. E. (2015). How smart, connected products are transforming companies. *Harvard Business Review, 93*(10), 96-16. Retrieved from http://search.ebscohost.com/login.aspx?direct=true&db=bth&AN=109338341&lang=zh-tw&site=ehost-live

Porter, M. E., & Millar, V. E. (1985). How information gives you competitive advantage. *Harvard Business Review, 63*(4), 61-78.

Ravichandran, T., & Lertwongsatien, C. (2005). Effect of Information Systems Resources and Capabilities on Firm Performance: A Resource-Based Perspective. *Journal of Management Information Systems, 21*(4),

237-276. doi:10.1080/07421222.2005.11045820

Respício, A., & Captivo, M. E. (2008). Marketing-production Interface through an Integrated DSS. *Journal of Decision Systems, 17*(1), 119-132.

Robinson, R. B., & Pearce, J. A. (1988). Planned Patterns of Strategic Behavior and Their Relationship to Business- Unit Performance. *Strategic Management Journal, 9*(1), 43-60. Retrieved from http://www.jstor.org/stable/2486001

Rouziès, D., & Hulland, J. (2014). Does marketing and sales integration always pay off? Evidence from a social capital perspective. *Journal of the Academy of Marketing Science, 42*(5), 511-527. doi:10.1007/s11747-014-0375-8

Slater, S. F., & Narver, J. C. (2000). Intelligence generation and superior customer value. *Journal of the Academy of Marketing Science, 28*(1), 120. doi:10.1177/0092070300281011

Slater, S. F., Olson, E. M., & Hult, G. T. M. (2006). The

Moderating Influence of Strategic Orientation on the Strategy Formation Capability-Performance Relationship. *Strategic Management Journal, 27*(12), 1221-1231. Retrieved from http://www.jstor.org/stable/20142409

Straub, D. W. (1989). Validating instruments in MIS research. *MIS Quarterly, 13*(2), 147-169.

Teece, D. J., Pisano, G., & Shuen, A. (1997). Dynamic Capabilities and Strategic Management. *Strategic Management Journal, 18*(7), 509-533. Retrieved from http://www.jstor.org/stable/3088148

Teo, H. H., Wei, K. K., & Benbasat, I. (2003). Predicting intention to adopt interganizaitonal linkages: an institutional perspective *MIS Quarterly, 27*(1), 19-49. Retrieved from http://search.ebscohost.com/login.aspx?direct=true&db=asr&AN=9284285&lang=zh-tw&site=ehost-live

Trainor, K. J., Krush, M. T., & Agnihotri, R. (2013).

Effects of relational proclivity and marketing intelligence on new product development. *Marketing Intelligence & Planning, 31*(7), 788-806. doi:http://dx.doi.org/10.1108/MIP-02-2013-0028

Tseng, S.-M. (2016). Knowledge management capability, customer relationship management, and service quality. *Journal of Enterprise Information Management, 29*(2), 202-221.

Vorhies, D. W., Morgan, R. E., & Autry, C. W. (2009). Product-market strategy and the marketing capabilities of the firm: impact on market effectiveness and cash flow performance. *Strategic Management Journal, 30*(12), 1310-1334.

Wang, Y., & Feng, H. (2012). Customer relationship management capabilities. *Management Decision, 50*(1), 115-129. doi:http://dx.doi.org/10.1108/00251741211194903

Weng, W. H. (2021, 28-30 May 2021). *Influential Components for the Sustainability of IoT-enabled*

Smart Systems: A Hierarchical Analysis. Paper presented at the 2021 IEEE 3rd Eurasia Conference on Biomedical Engineering, Healthcare and Sustainability (ECBIOS).

Weng, W. H., & Lin, W. T. (2014). A scenario analysis of wearable interface technology foresight. *AIS Electronic Library (AISeL).*

Weng, W. H., & Lin, W. T. (2015). A Mobile Computing Technology Foresight Study with Scenario Planning Approach. *International Journal of Electronic Commerce Studies, 6*(2), 223-231. doi:10.7903/ijecs.1242

Wu, J.-J. (2004). Influence of market orientation and strategy on travel industry performance: an empirical study of e-commerce in Taiwan. *Tourism Management, 25*(3), 357-365. doi:10.1016/s0261-5177(03)00144-4

Xie, K., Wu, Y., Xiao, J., & Hu, Q. (2016). Value co-creation between firms and customers: The role of big data-based cooperative assets. *Information & Management, 53*(8), 1034-1048. doi:10.1016/j.im.2016.06.003

Yu, X., Nguyen, B., & Chen, Y. (2016). Internet of things capability and alliance. *Internet Research, 26*(2), 402-434.

Zancul, E. d. S., Takey, S. M., Barquet, A. P. B., Kuwabara, L. H., Cauchick Miguel, P. A., & Rozenfeld, H. (2016). Business process support for IoT based product-service systems (PSS). *Business Process Management Journal, 22*(2), 305-323.

Chapter 3
Big Data Analytics and Supply Chain Competence

Abstract

Recent advancements in big data analytics have invoked tremendous attention from both academics and industries. Many researchers refer that the adoption and application of big data analytics could lead to performance impact to organizations, and therefore further affect organizational adoption intention of this technology. However, few researches study the association between business strategy and big data analytics adoption. Furthermore, the role of firms' functional activities such as supply chain operations has seldom been addressed in the adoption considerations of big data analytics. In this research, empirical data from enterprises were collected and analyzed to assess the impact of business strategy on big data analytics adoption and the possible effect of supply chain competence in the linkage. The results supported our hypotheses and the implications for management decisions are elaborated.

Keywords: Business strategy, big data analytics, supply chain competence, technology adoption intention, information processing view, ambidexterity

1. Introduction

Big data is characterized by scholars and practitioners with three Vs: Volume, or the large amount of data that either consume huge storage or entail of large number of data records; Velocity, which is the frequency or the speed of data generation, data delivery and data change; and Variety, to highlight the property that data are generated from a large variety of sources and formats, and contain multidimensional data fields including structured and unstructured data (Fosso Wamba, Akter, Edwards, Chopin, & Gnanzou, 2015; Hashem et al., 2015; McAfee & Brynjolfsson, 2012; Weng & Lin, 2013; Weng & Weng, 2013). Big data analytics refers to the methods, algorithms, middleware and systems to discover, retrieve, store, analyze and present big data, in order to generate the fourth V: Value for business.

The development of big data analytics is a response to the world of fast accumulating data, such as social media data, electronic commerce data, geographical data, multimedia streaming data, and many others generated from personal and organizational applications. Other emerging technologies, such as cloud computing and internet of things, also enhanced the needs of big data analytics. For example, with the rapid pace of development in cloud computing, data centers of both public clouds and private clouds are continuing to accumulate enormous volumes of data; as a result, big data analytics and its applications are becoming ever more noticed (Agrawal, Das, & Abbadi, 2011; Hashem et al., 2015; Weng & Lin, 2014).

While the influences of big data analytics on enterprise performance were explored in previous studies (Fosso Wamba et al., 2015), the essential issue of whether firms will adopt big data analytics remains unresolved, and factors associated with enterprise adoption intention of big data analytics have not been comprehensively investigated. Furthermore, possible relationships between big data adoption intention and firms' business level strategies and functional level strategies are also rare in the literature.

Studies of organizational information processing theory (Galbraith, 1974; Tushman & Nadler, 1978) have shown that the uncertainty that firms encounter when formulating and executing business strategy is an important factor for firms' adoption of innovative information technologies (Koo, Koh, & Nam, 2004; Porter & Millar, 1985; Smith, McKeen, & Singh, 2007). This result leads to the speculation that business strategy pursuit is associated with big data analytics adoption intention. Furthermore, the high level concept of business strategy needs to be implemented and realized in efficient functional level activities such as human resource management, research and development, production, marketing, sales, customer services, and supply chain operations (S. Li, Ragu-Nathan, Ragu-Nathan, & Subba Rao, 2006). Among these functional level activities, this paper focuses on the role of supply chain operations for several reasons. First, the growing data volume in supply chain operations: Supply chain activities need to collaborate with other trading partners across corporate boundary. Supply chains link value chains of participating parties (Cheung, Myers, & Mentzer, 2010; Cook, Heiser, & Sengupta, 2011). Second, the increasing data velocity in supply chain operations: Many organizations are gradually aware of that they must compete, as part of a supply chain against other supply chains, to quickly reflect customers' changing demands (I.-L. Wu & Chuang, 2010). Finally, the expanding data variety in supply chain operations: Supply chain management is closely integrated with more and more other functions such as production, marketing and information systems (Dong, Xu, & Zhu, 2009; Kozlenkova, Hult, Lund, Mena, & Kekec, 2015). Therefore, this research intends to investigate the linkage between business strategy and big data analytics adoption, and the effect of supply chain competence in this linkage.

The paper begins with a review of the relevant literature about the relationships between business strategy, supply chain competence and big data analytics. Then it proposes a model which links these variables. Following that, the model is tested using a sample of large Taiwanese companies with operations in China. Finally, the findings are presented along with the managerial implications of the study, its limitations and recommendations for future work.

2. Literature Review and Hypotheses Development
2.1 Business Strategy and Supply Chain Competence

Porter's framework for business strategy of competition is one of the most widely accepted typology of business competition models (A. Miller & Dess, 1993; Porter, 1980). Porter's research in industrial economics suggested two fundamental types of generic business level strategies for achieving above average rates of return: cost leadership and differentiation (Porter, 1980, 1985). Porter proposed that to succeed in business, a firm must pursue one or more of these generic business strategies, and that a firm's strategic choice eventually determines its competitiveness and profitability (D. Miller, 1988). Other scholars argued that the two types of business strategies are not strictly mutual exclusive. Firms adopting cost leadership strategy may seek to deliver distinctive products or services under the main theme of low cost thinking. Firms with differentiation strategy could also attempt low cost operations as long as the uniqueness of products or services is maintained (Hill, 1988; Murray, 1988).

The successful implementation of the business strategies relies on making right decisions on core functions of a firm, such as human resource management, production, marketing, research and development, sales, information systems, and supply chain management.

These functions form a value chain and all have a role in lowering the cost structure and increasing the value of products through differentiation (Porter, 1985). A firm's ability to acquire superior functional efficiency, including supply chain competence, will determine if its product offering is differentiated from that of its competitors, and if it has a low cost structure simultaneously. Firms that increase the utility consumers get from their offerings through differentiation, while at the same time lowering their cost structure, can create more value than their rivals, and will acquire a competitive advantage, superior profitability, and profit growth (Hill, 1988; Huo, Qi, Wang, & Zhao, 2014).

Cost leadership strategy is pursued through low cost operations in each segment of supply chain activities, including production scheduling, demand management, sourcing and procurement, inventory management, distribution and delivery (Huan, Sheoran, & Wang, 2004; Lockamy & McCormack, 2004). For differentiation strategy, the principal thinking in these operations are geared towards the design and delivery of distinctive products and services. Differentiation may also eventuate in unique methods or channels of sourcing or delivery, in innovative manufacturing processes or inventory operations in a supply chain (Wagner, Grosse-Ruyken, & Erhun, 2012). Thus, the following two hypotheses are proposed:

H1a. Cost leadership strategy pursuit is positively associated with supply chain competence.

H1b. Differentiation strategy pursuit is positively associated with supply chain competence.

Although H1a and H1b both hypothesize positive effects on supply chain competence from two different business strategies, the means through which the two strategies are linked to supply chain competence are quite different. Differentiation strategy pursuit is linked to supply chain competence through effectiveness in product innovation and customization, whereas cost leadership strategy pursuit is linked to supply chain competence through efficiency in operations (G. Kim & Huh, 2015). Even though both strategies have a positive impact on supply chain competence, differentiation strategy pursuit is considered to have a stronger relationship with supply chain competence than cost leadership strategy pursuit will have. Because differentiation strategy pursuit represents an approach to product or service innovation, whether through the development of unique product features or through the enablement of business innovations which explore opportunities, it requires the support of highly efficient supply chain operations which are responsive to changing customer preferences. These supply chain operations need to react to unique customer experiences with speed and flexibility. To sustain in competition, the differentiators will always need to be a step ahead, looking for the next uniqueness enhancing innovation. The differentiators are therefore more likely to require promptness and flexibility in supply chain operations. Furthermore, the impact that the introduction of a radical product or business innovation has on the supply chain activities of a firm is likely to exceed that of the implementation of a cost efficient solution that is more common in an industry regardless of the efficiency that it brings (Leidner, Lo, & Preston, 2011). Thus the following is hypothesized:

H1c. The relationship between differentiation strategy pursuit and supply chain competence will be stronger than the relationship between cost leadership strategy pursuit and supply chain competence.

2.2 Business Strategy and Big Data Analytics

A business strategy concerns the competitive positioning, market segmentation and industry environment of a company (Porter, 1980). To survive, grow and sustain, a firm needs to constantly monitor its internal and external status for possible changes. Thus the formulation and execution of a business strategy rely heavily on the collection, extraction, analyze, interpretation and prediction on internal and external status data of a company, in order to make accurate managerial decisions (Claver-Cortés, Pertusa-Ortega, & Molina-Azorín, 2012; McAfee & Brynjolfsson, 2012).

From the information processing view (Galbraith, 1974), an organization is an imperfect decision-making system due to incomplete knowledge. Therefore, firms seek to systematically progress to support decision-making when facing increased uncertainty. Uncertainty is associated with inadequate information related to decision-making. The competitive information extracted from big data comprises information of sales and marketing, research and development, manufacturing and production, finance and accounting, human resources, and similar data from the other competitors (Tushman & Nadler, 1978). This information can be acquired and processed by applying big data analytics.

Organizing and leveraging these big data analytics from functional operations up the hierarchy and systematically using it to ascertain the competitive situation along with the formation of business strategies involve the essence of the managerial decisions on competition (Mathews, 2016). Furthermore, business strategies of most organizations are frequently a combination of their intended strategies and the emergent strategies (Mintzberg, 1985). Firm leaders need to analyze the process of emergence and to make strategy adjustment when appropriate (Mintzberg & Waters, 1985). For this purpose, big data analytics could also serve as the tool to facilitate the strategic decisions to be accurately aligned with competition changes (Akter, Wamba, Gunasekaran, Dubey, & Childe, 2016; Janssen, van der Voort, & Wahyudi, 2017).

Big data analytics is used to store, convert, transmit and analyze large quantities of dynamic, diversified data, which may be structured or unstructured data, for the purpose of business benefit (Borkar, Carey, & Li, 2012; Chen, Chiang, & Storey, 2012). Big Data processing requires tools and techniques that leverage the combination of various IT resources: processing power, memory, storage, network, and end user devices to access the processed outcomes. Efficient analytical tools are developed to process the large amounts of unstructured heterogeneous data collected continuously in various formats such as text, picture, audio, video, log file and others (Babiceanu & Seker, 2016). Current examples of such tools include the Hadoop Distributed File System (HDFS) (Shafer, Rixner, & Cox, 2010), the parallel processing system MapReduce (Glushkova, Jovanovic, & Abelló, 2017), the non-relational database system NoSQL (Stonebraker, 2010), and others. These tools provide processing functionality for big data which are beyond the application scope of traditional data mining and business analytics tools.

Big data analytics with the 3Vs (Volume + Velocity + Variety) provides a clear picture of product use, showing instantly which features customers prefer or dislike, by means of the increased volume, velocity and variety of data collected from customer responses. An example is the effects of word of mouth created by a large number of online visitors on consumer's purchase preference for manufacturers and retailers (Wien & Olsen, 2017; Xie, Wu, Xiao, & Hu, 2016). By analyzing and comparing more dimensions of usage patterns, firms can do much precise customer segmentation, by industry, geography, age, income, and even more granular attributes. Decision makers can apply this deeper knowledge to tailor special offers or after-sale service packages, create features for certain segments, and develop more sophisticated pricing strategies that better match price and value at the segment or even the individual customer level (Qi, Zhang, Jeon, & Zhou,

2016). These price and value analytics further forms the basis for decisions of differentiation and cost structure.

For companies pursuing cost leadership strategy, cost analytics of all levels is more accurately analyzed to maintain a viable leading cost structure. For firms pursuing differentiation strategy, customer preference analytics determines the need to differentiate their products against the need to keep their cost structure under control in order to offer a product at a competitive price (Xie et al., 2016).

In summary, we propose the following hypotheses:

H2a. Cost leadership strategy pursuit is positively associated with big data analytics adoption intention.

H2b. Differentiation strategy pursuit is positively associated with big data analytics adoption intention.

Technology is one of the most prominent factors influencing the rules of competition (Porter, 1980). Through the help of technology use, a firm creates products and services that can differentiate itself from its rivals or to produce at a lower cost (D. Miller, 1988; Porter & Millar, 1985). However, while H2a and H2b both hypothesize positive effects on big data analytics adoption intention from two different business strategies, the purposes for which the two strategies utilize big data analytics are relatively different. A firm with a differentiation strategy uses big data analytics to achieve product uniqueness through innovation or customization. Identifying distinctive innovative features and customer preferences is mainly an exploratory activity. On the other hand, a firm with a cost leadership strategy uses big data analytics for possible higher efficiency and lower cost, which is primarily exploitative (March, 1991). Firms placing great emphasis on differentiation strategies are likely to rely more strongly on the functionality of big data analytics because of the higher information uncertainty and diversity in exploration than in exploitation. Differentiation strategy pursuit represents an approach to product or service innovation, whether through the development of unique product features or through the enablement of business innovations which explore opportunities, it requires the support of highly effective predictive analytics which realize changing customer preferences. These business analytics are required to analyze and learn the unique customer experiences with accuracy and flexibility. To sustain in competition, the differentiators constantly need to watch for the next unique innovation. Therefore, the differentiators are more likely to require the outcomes of big data analytics. In this regard, the following is hypothesized:

H2c. The relationship between differentiation strategy pursuit and big data analytics adoption intention will be stronger than the relationship between cost leadership strategy pursuit and big data analytics adoption intention.

2.3 Supply Chain Competence and Big Data Analytics

Supply chain operations generate and utilize large-scale heterogeneous data with time-varying nature (Gunasekaran, Patel, & Tirtiroglu, 2001). The timely and accurate flow of information is a necessity for successful supply chain operations (White, Daniel, & Mohdzain, 2005). The evolution of big data analytics is expected to transform enterprises' managerial paradigm, including supply chain management (Waller & Fawcett, 2013). The relationships between supply chain competence and information technology adoption have been widely studied. The findings suggest that IT advancement and IT alignment can facilitate the development of supply chain competence (DeGroote & Marx, 2013; Qrunfleh & Tarafdar, 2014; Vijayasarathy, 2010; F. Wu, Yeniyurt, Kim, & Cavusgil, 2006). These results lead to the conjecture of the association between supply chain competence and big data analytics (Schoenherr & Speier-Pero, 2015; Waller & Fawcett, 2013). The possible association between supply chain competence and big data analytics adoption has thus become a crucial topic to both academics and practitioners (Hazen, Boone, Ezell, & Jones-Farmer, 2014). For enterprises, big data analytics adoption may facilitate and enhance information processing and exchange. Big data analytics can undertake real-time and high-complexity analytics of vast amounts of operational data, to help enterprises perform decision-making within critical timeframe (Bryant, Katz, & Lazowska, 2008). The 3Vs capability of big data analytics is well aligned for responding to the requirement of supply chain operations (McAfee & Brynjolfsson, 2012; Waller & Fawcett, 2013). Therefore, big data analytics adoption in a firm is expected to produce significant results concerning enhancement of supply chain competence.

The efficiency considerations in supply chain operations mainly centers around time efficiency, cost efficiency and flexibility (Beamon, 1999; Gunasekaran,

Patel, & McGaughey, 2004). The time efficiency in supply chain includes reducing lead time, response time and delivery time of products and services. The cost efficiency consideration in supply chain comprises lowering the costs of materials, inventory, distribution and transportation, and information exchange among various sites in supply chain. The flexibility of supply chain is enhanced by instant adjustment to changes from customer requirements, supplier and distributer conditions, and any other possible events such as natural disasters (Beamon, 1999; Gunasekaran et al., 2004).

The 3Vs capability of big data is desired for efficient supply chain operations. The efficiency in supply chain operations is supported by prompt interchange of status data among parties participating in the supply chain. As the supply chain competence keep enhancing, data volume may grow from more detailed information regarding price, quantity, items sold, time of day, date, customer data, and inventory at more locations and a more dispersed level. Data velocity is also increased because of the frequent updates of sales orders, inventory status and transportation time. Data variety is amplified since the attributes of products, channels of procurement and methods of delivering products and services become more versatile (Robak, Franczyk, & Robak, 2013). These 3Vs of big data are also amplified by joining applications of other emerging technologies such as cloud computing, RFID, and Internet of Things in the supply chain (Angeles, 2005; Atzori, Iera, & Morabito, 2010; Cegielski, Allison Jones-Farmer, Wu, & Hazen, 2012). Thus to pursue supply chain competence, firms will intend to adopt big data analytics.

Therefore, the hypothesis of this research suggests that:

H3. Supply chain competence is positively associated with big data analytics adoption intention.

Based on our proposed hypotheses, the research framework is illustrated in Figure 1.

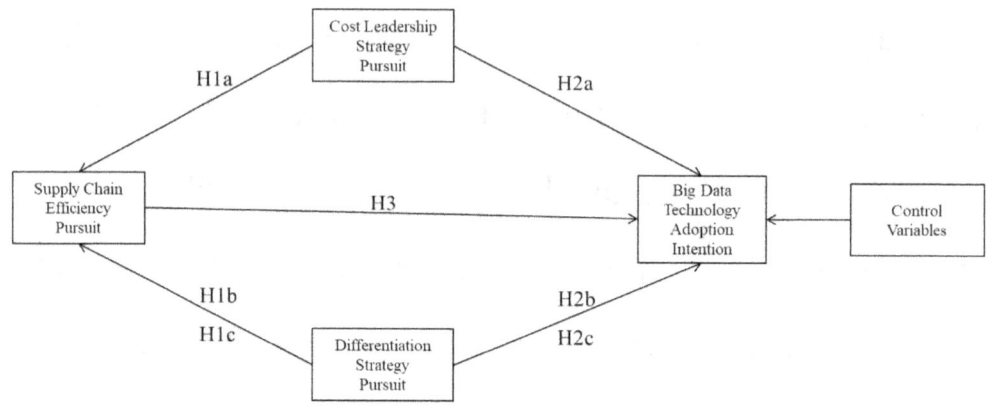

Figure 1   Research framework

3. Research Method

3.1 Survey Instrument

The survey instrument was developed using questions derived from the literature on Porter's competitive strategies, the supply chain competence framework, and big data analytics adoption intention discussed previously. We operationalized the study variables by using multi-item reflective measures on a 7-point scale (Jarvis, MacKenzie, & Podsakoff, 2003).

The construct of cost leadership strategy pursuit was measured using four items that reflect the extent to which a firm pursues a cost-oriented strategy. First, cost leadership refers to the generation of higher margins than those of competitors by achieving lower operation costs. Firms with a cost leadership strategy often have highly stable product lines and a strong emphasis on profit and budget controls (D. Miller, 1988). Second, pursuing of cost leadership is often reflected in price competitiveness (Dess & Davis, 1984; Robinson & Pearce, 1988). The third item was the economic scale. A firm can gain a cost advantage through economies of scale or superior manufacturing processes (Porter, 1980, 1985). Finally, larger firms with greater access to resources are more likely to take advantage of cost leadership strategy through development of lower cost products, whereas smaller firms are often forced to compete using highly differentiated products and services in a niche market (Wright, 1987).

The differentiation strategy pursuit construct was measured using four items that reflect the extent to which a firm pursues a differentiation strategy. Differentiation entails being unique or distinct from competitors, for example, by providing superior information, prices, distribution channels, and prestige to the customer (Porter, 1980). Differentiation prevents a business from competitive rivalry, insulating it from competitive forces that reduce margins (Kotha & Vadlamani, 1995). Extending Porter's competitive strategy framework, Miller distinguished differentiation strategies based on innovation from those based on marketing (D. Miller, 1988). These propositions form two items included in the construct. Differentiation strategies based on innovation may create a dynamic environment or a distinct business model in which it is difficult for competitors to predict and react. This unpredictability may provide the innovator a substantial advantage over its competitors (D. Miller, 1988; Robinson & Pearce, 1988).

The construct of supply chain competence was measured using six items. Respondents rated their intensity of pursuing supply chain competence over the time frame of past few years. Beamon (1999) proposed a framework for measuring supply chain competence. The framework included the measurement of resources, output, and flexibility as the strategic goals of supply chain operations. The key measuring variables included cost, activity time, customer responsiveness, and flexibility. These variables have been recognized as direct and observable measures of supply chain practice. Firms in a supply chain achieve efficiency by lowering operational costs, reducing inventory, promoting flexibility, ensuring on-time deliveries, and minimizing shortages of critical resources. These objectives relate to all parties in a buyer–supplier relationship, and therefore, can represent the efficiency of the supply chain operations (Gunasekaran et al., 2004; Gunasekaran et al., 2001).

The big data analytics adoption intention construct served as the dependent variable and was measured using three items by the subjects' responses to whether, if given the opportunity, they would adopt big data analytics for their respective firm within one year's time. To facilitate this measurement, we followed the guidelines established by Ajzen (1991) and adapted items employed by Venkatesh and Bala (2008). These items measure user intention in the context of the technology acceptance model (Davis, 1989).

All items for this study were assessed with a 7-point Likert scale ranging from "strongly disagree" to "strongly agree." In addition, we use firm size, IT department size and industry sector as control variables, as these factors have been noted in several studies to affect intention to adopt information technologies (Liu, Ke, Wei, Gu, & Chen, 2010; Teo, Wei, & Benbasat, 2003). Table 1 presents the items used to measure each of the independent and dependent construct variables.

Table 1 Constructs and items used in the survey

Construct and item description (1 – strongly disagree; 7 – strongly agree)

CLS: Cost leadership strategy pursuit

CLS1: We provide low cost products or services based on operational efficiency.

CLS2: We deliver products or services with lower price than competitors.

CLS3: We provide products or services with economy of scale.

CLS4: We develop our products or services with lower cost than our competitors.

DFS: Differentiation strategy pursuit

DFS1: We deliver products or services with distinctive business model.

DFS2: We differentiate our products or services based on innovation.

DFS3: We deliver products or services with superior functionality to our competitors.

DFS4: We differentiate our products or services based on effective marketing.

SCC: Supply chain competence

SCC1: We delivery products or services on time.

SCC2: Reducing lead time is crucial to us in our supply chain operations.

SCC3: We respond promptly to changes of customer requirements.

SCC4: Lack of critical resources is effectively avoided in our supply chain operations.

SCC5: Inventory and logistics flexibility is above average in our supply chain operations.

SCC6: Reducing the cost of our supply chain operations is important to us.

BDA: Big data analytics adoption intention

BDA1: If we have the ability to adopt any big data analytics for our company, we will do so.

BDA2: If we have access to any big data analytics, we would want to use it.

BDA3: My company plans to adopt big data analytics within one year.

Control Variables (rescaled)

Firm Size: Total number of employees.

IT Size: Total number of IT staffs.

Industry: Industry sectors of firms. 1 for service firms and 0 for manufacturing firms.

3.2 Sample and Data Collection

Empirical data for testing the hypothesized relationships were obtained by conducting a survey of large Taiwanese companies. A questionnaire developed in accordance with Table 2 was implemented as the survey instrument. It was pretested in an iterative manner among a sample of 15 executives and managers. The questionnaire items were revised on the basis of the results of the expert interviews and refined through pretesting to establish content validity. The pretesting focused on instrument clarity, question wording, and validity. During the pretesting, members of the testing sample were invited to comment on the questions and wording of the questionnaire. The comments of these respondents then provided a basis for revisions to the construct measures.

China Credit Information Service, Inc. publishes comprehensive data of the 1,000 largest corporations in Taiwan with operations in China. Most of these companies are public listed corporations with global transactions. After the pretesting and revision, survey invitations and the questionnaires were mailed to these 1,000 companies. Follow-up letters were sent approximately 15 days after the initial mailing. Data were collected through responses from executives and managers of the companies. Data collection was completed in two months. In total, 201 valid questionnaires were obtained, with a valid response rate of 20.1%. We compared respondent and non-respondent firms in terms of industry, size (number of employees) and revenue. These comparisons did not show any significant differences, suggesting no response bias. Table 2 shows the profile of the final sample list.

Table 2 Profile of the final sampling firms

	Count	% of sample
Number of employees		
Under 100	33	16%
100~1,000	64	32%
1,000~5,000	59	29%
5,000~10,000	35	17%
Above 10,000	10	5%
Total	201	100%
Number of IT Staffs		
Under 5	66	33%
6~10	31	15%
11~20	49	24%
21~50	34	17%
Above 50	21	10%
Total	201	100%
Industry sectors		
Manufacturing	93	46%
Services	108	54%
Total	201	100%

4. Results

Our goal was to investigate the impact of business strategy pursuit on big data analytics adoption intention, mediated by a firm's supply chain competence. The empirical results were expected to demonstrate that pursuing business strategy, such as cost leadership strategy and differentiation strategy, influences the adoption intention of big data analytics. The results were also expected to verify the mediating role of supply chain competence on the link between business strategy pursuit and big data analytics adoption intention. Finally, the results were used to test the relationship between business strategy pursuit and supply chain competence.

4.1 Reliability and Validity

The reliability of the survey instrument was tested by using Cronbach's alpha (Cronbach, 1951) to assess the internal consistency of the CLS, DFS, SCC and BDA constructs listed in Table 1. Cronbach's alpha tests the interrelationship among the items composing a construct to determine if the items measure a single construct. Nunnally and Bernstein (1994) recommended a threshold alpha value of .7. Cicchetti et al. (2011)

suggested the following reliability guidelines for determining significance: α < .70 (unacceptable), .70 ≤ α < .80 (fair), .80 ≤ α < .90 (good), and α > .90 (excellent).

Content validity (Straub, 1989) refers to the extent to which the instrument measures what it is designed to measure. Most of the measures used in the study were adopted from relevant studies. Although basing the study on the established literature provided a considerable level of validity, the study's validity was further improved by pre-testing the instrument on a panel of experts comprising 15 business executives and supply chain managers.

To assess convergent and discriminant validity, the items that were used to measure the CLS, DFS, SCC and BDA constructs were subjected to principal components analysis with varimax rotation. The Bartlett test of sphericity and the Kaiser–Meyer–Olkin measure of sampling adequacy were conducted to ensure that the sample was satisfactory and confirm the appropriateness of proceeding with further data analysis.

Table 3 summarizes the descriptive statistics and results of the reliability and validity tests. The reliability of the instrument was examined using composite reliability estimates by employing Cronbach's α. All the coefficients exceeded Nunnally's recommended level (0.70) of internal consistency (Cicchetti et al., 2011; Nunnally & Bernstein, 1994). In addition, factor analysis was performed to confirm the construct validity. The results supported the constructs of our research model. The discriminant validity was confirmed since items for each constructs loaded on to single factors with all loadings greater than 0.8. These results confirm that each of the construct in our hypothesized model is unidimensional and factorially distinct, and that all items used to operationalize a construct is loaded onto a single factor.

Table 3 Descriptive statistics and reliability and validity test

Construct	Item	Mean	SD	Cronbach's alpha	Cronbach's alpha if item deleted	Factor loading on single factor
CLS	CLS1	3.716	1.521	0.952	0.956	0.912
	CLS2	3.597	1.460		0.978	0.855
	CLS3	3.657	1.320		0.905	0.909
	CLS4	3.677	1.351		0.908	0.993
DFS	DFS1	4.552	1.371	0.905	0.893	0.854
	DFS2	4.393	1.375		0.857	0.921
	DFS3	4.308	1.579		0.889	0.866
	DFS4	4.214	1.456		0.870	0.895
SCC	SCP1	4.507	1.460	0.920	0.911	0.815
	SCP2	4.935	1.338		0.901	0.870
	SCP3	4.612	1.330		0.901	0.869
	SCP4	4.552	1.330		0.905	0.847
	SCP5	4.423	1.465		0.909	0.827
	SCP6	4.547	1.396		0.904	0.849
BDA	BDA1	4.451	1.619	0.892	0.768	0.952
	BDA2	4.506	1.652		0.760	0.956
	BDA3	3.998	1.478		0.972	0.806

Table 4 presents the results of factor analysis. A four-factor structure emerged with all predefined indicators loading on to their respective constructs, which thereby affirmed convergent validity and unidimensionality of the constructs. The model explained 79.830% of the variance.

Table 4 Factor analysis

Construct	Item	Factor1	Factor2	Factor3	Factor4
CLS	CLS1	**.847**	.337	.160	-.019
	CLS2	**.789**	.105	.291	.239
	CLS3	**.924**	.252	.253	.121
	CLS4	**.920**	.291	.225	.072
DFS	DFS1	.255	**.747**	.288	.109
	DFS2	.245	**.834**	.282	.133
	DFS3	.217	**.787**	.267	.146
	DFS4	.296	**.745**	.388	.082
SCC	SCP1	.230	.205	**.756**	.084
	SCP2	.114	.311	**.803**	.099
	SCP3	.131	.227	**.837**	.069
	SCP4	.249	.144	**.816**	.036
	SCP5	.236	.235	**.723**	.217
	SCP6	.164	.271	**.754**	.217
BDA	BDA1	.096	.093	.156	**.927**
	BDA2	.102	.046	.121	**.939**
	BDA3	.073	.179	.107	**.880**

We also assessed discriminant validity on the basis of the construct correlation. Table 5 summarizes the correlations among different factors. The tests indicated acceptable results with respect to discriminant validity.

Table 5   Construct correlation

Construct	1	2	3	4	5	6	7
1. CLS	1						
2. DFS	0.625**	1					
3. SCC	0.556**	0.642**	1				
4. BDA	0.272**	0.306**	0.324**	1			
5. Firm Size	-0.031	-0.048	-0.035	0.208**	1		
6. IT Size	0.185**	0.085	0.048	0.111	0.357**	1	
7. Industry	-0.024	-0.026	-0.061	0.101	-0.027	-0.144*	1

$*p < 0.05$, $**p < 0.01$

4.2 Tests of Hypotheses

Multiple linear regression analysis was performed using SPSS version 21 to test our hypotheses for significance. Table 6 summarizes the test results regarding the parameter estimates and p-values of the hypothesized model in Figure 1. We also included firm size, IT department size and industry sector as control variables in the analysis.

Table 6 Tests results of the hypothesized model

Explanatory variable	Dependent variable					
	SCC		BDA model without SCC		BDA model with SCC	
	Estimate	P-value	Estimate	P-value	Estimate	P-value
CLS	0.237	0.000***	0.154	0.018*	0.091	0.367
DFS	0.444	0.000***	0.266	0.005**	0.154	0.144
SCC					0.255	0.019*
Firm size			0.079	0.102	0.073	0.112
IT size			0.008	0.979	0.055	0.856
Industry			0.117	0.080	0.127	0.064
R^2	0.451		0.168		0.191	

*$p < 0.05$, **$p < 0.01$, ***$p < 0.001$

The results in Table 6 supported the hypotheses H1a, H1b and H3, that is, the direct effects of CLS on SCC, DFS on SCC and SCC on BDA. In the links of CLS on

BDA of hypothesis H2a and DFS on BDA of hypothesis H2b, the direct effects were not found, instead, complete mediation effects of SCC in the links were found. This indicates that business strategy pursuit is positively related to big data analytics adoption intention through mediation effect rather than direct effect. The test procedure concerning mediation follows the suggestion of Baron and Kenny (1986). We compared the proposed mediation model with an alternative direct effect model without SCC variable. The test results show that positive relationships exist between CLS and SCC ($\beta= 0.237$, $p < 0.001$), between DFS and SCC ($\beta= 0.444$, $p < 0.001$), and between SCC and BDA ($\beta= 0.255$, $p < 0.05$). Furthermore, the significant relationships between CLS and BDA ($\beta= 0.154$, $p < 0.05$) and between DFS and BDA ($\beta= 0.266$, $p < 0.01$) in the direct effect model is not significant in the model with mediation. Taking into account these results as a whole, we thus conclude that the effect of business strategy pursuit on big data analytics adoption intention is completely mediated by supply chain competence (Baron & Kenny, 1986). The effects of paths are summarized in Table 7.

Table 7　Effects of paths in the hypothesized model

Hypothesis	path	Effect from test results
H1a	CLS → SCC	Direct effect supported
H1b	DFS → SCC	Direct effect supported
H2a	CLS → BDA	Direct effect not supported Complete mediation of SCC supported
H2b	DFS → BDA	Direct effect not supported Complete mediation of SCC supported
H3	SCC → BDA	Direct effect supported

For hypotheses H1c and H2c, we used hierarchical linear regression to test the differences in the effects of differentiation strategy pursuit and cost leadership strategy pursuit on supply chain competence and big data analytics adoption intention.

H1c stated that the relationship between differentiation strategy pursuit (DFS) and supply chain competence (SCC) will be stronger than the relationship between cost leadership strategy pursuit (CLS) and supply chain competence (SCC). The test results indicated that the standardized beta is 0.254 for the cost leadership strategy's relationship with supply chain competence and 0.483 for the differentiation strategy. The analysis showed a change in R^2 of 0.142 (F change = 51.382, p = 0.000) when the differentiation strategy was added to the model with the cost leadership strategy (original R^2 of 0.309). This signifies that the differentiation strategy explains above and beyond what the cost leadership strategy can explain for supply chain competence, thereby supporting H1c.

Likewise, H2c stated that the relationship between differentiation strategy pursuit (DFS) and big data analytics adoption intention (BDA) will be stronger than the relationship between cost leadership strategy pursuit

(CLS) and big data analytics adoption intention (BDA). The test results indicated that the standardized beta is 0.134 for the cost leadership strategy's relationship with big data analytics adoption intention and 0.236 for the differentiation strategy. The analysis showed a change in R^2 of 0.034 (F change = 7.940, p = 0.005) when the differentiation strategy was added to the model with the cost leadership strategy (original R^2 of 0.134). This signifies that the differentiation strategy explains above and beyond what the cost leadership strategy can explain for big data analytics adoption intention, thereby supporting H2c.

We further compared firms with different strategic orientations using ANOVA test with Scheffé's method. The firms were classified as ambidexter, differentiator, cost leader and unspecific firms. Firms were classified as ambidexter if their ratings for both the differentiation strategy pursuit (DFS) and cost leadership strategy pursuit (CLS) were, on average, above the sample means for differentiation and cost leadership, respectively. Otherwise, they were classified as either differentiator or cost leader depending on the strategy on which they rated higher than average. The rest of firms were classified as unspecific. Table 8 summarized the classification of firms with their average ratings on supply chain competence (SCC) and big data analytics adoption intention (BDA).

Table 8   Classification of firms by strategy types

Firm type	Criteria		Count	% of sample	SCC		BDA	
	DFS	CLS			Mean	SD	Mean	SD
Ambidexter	high	high	71	35.3%	5.263	0.788	4.903	1.073
Differentiator	high	low	27	13.4%	4.660	1.061	4.425	1.598
Cost leader	low	high	46	22.9%	4.359	0.632	3.946	1.642
Unspecific	low	low	57	28.4%	3.927	1.489	3.840	1.343
Total			201	100.0%	4.596	1.172	4.318	1.438

To determine whether the differences in the means of SCC and BDA for each group of firm strategies were statistically significant, we used an ANOVA test with

Scheffé's method. The Scheffé method is used for post hoc multiple comparisons and is suitable whether sample sizes are equal or unequal. Table 9 summarizes the results of the comparison.

Table 9   Comparison of firms by strategy types

Firm type A	Firm type B	SCC Mean (A – B)	SE	P-value	BDA Mean (A – B)	SE	P-value
Ambidexter	Differentiator	0.602	0.236	0.093	0.479	0.310	0.497
	Cost leader	0.904	0.198	0.000***	0.957	0.259	0.004**
	Unspecific	1.336	0.186	0.000***	1.064	0.244	0.000***
Differentiator	Cost leader	0.302	0.253	0.701	0.478	0.332	0.558
	Unspecific	0.734	0.244	0.031*	0.585	0.320	0.344
Cost leader	Unspecific	0.432	0.207	0.230	0.107	0.271	0.985

*$p < 0.05$, **$p < 0.01$, ***$p < 0.001$

Results from this analysis revealed that the mean SCC difference between ambidexter and differentiator organizations was not statistically significant, but that the difference between ambidexters and cost leaders was statistically significant, as was the difference between ambidexters and unspecific firms and the difference between differentiators and unspecific firms. The mean BDA difference between ambidexters and differentiators was not statistically significant, but that the difference between ambidexters and cost leaders was statistically significant, as was the difference between ambidexters and unspecific firms.

5. Discussion and Conclusions
5.1 Research Implications

This study investigated the impact of a firm's business strategy pursuit on big data analytics adoption intention, and tested the possible mediating role of supply chain competence. Supporting the research hypotheses, the first critical insight we obtained from our empirical results is that the link between a firm's business strategy pursuit and its intention of big data analytics adoption was completely mediated by the supply chain competence of the firm. This result is observed for both cost leadership strategy and differentiation strategy. In other words, the link between business strategy pursuit and big data analytics adoption intention is not direct, but indirect instead. By adopting a mediating framework in this study, we isolated the specific effects by which business strategy pursuit are linked to big data analytics adoption intention. This finding suggests that pursuing business level strategy alone does not directly link to innovative technology adoption intention. Functional level efficiency of firms may play a key role in the link. This result provides valuable evaluation reference for firms making management decision in adopting innovative information technologies.

The second observation is that the direct effect of supply chain competence on big data analytics adoption intention was positive and significant. This suggests that supply chain competence has more of direct impact on big data adoption intention than business strategy pursuit. From the information processing view (Galbraith, 1974;

Tushman & Nadler, 1978), this finding indicates that the perceived complexity and uncertainty for supply chain operations are significant for firms (Waller & Fawcett, 2013), and the information requirement involved may impel firms for big data analytics adoption. A managerial implication here is that a supply chain operation unit of a firm is good at understanding the outside environment because of its participation and collaboration with the other organizations in the supply chain. Therefore, a supply chain operation unit in a firm becomes critical for a firm to make its strategic decisions fit with its surroundings, including technology adoption decisions. As the data volume, data velocity and data variety in supply chain operations continue advancing, the demand for big data analytics may also keep evolving. The intensity of supply chain competence is therefore a significant predictor for big data analytics utilization.

Our findings also provide evidence that for both cost leadership strategy and differentiation strategy, there is a positive relation between business strategy pursuit and supply chain competence. This result supports the theoretical literature on the relationship of business level strategies and functional level strategies (Nandakumar, Ghobadian, & O'Regan, 2011; Pagell & Krause, 2002; Williams, D'Souza, Rosenfeldt, & Kassaee, 1995). Our results also indicate that supply chain competence influences big data analytics adoption intention significantly regardless of which business strategy a firm chooses to pursue. Both cost leadership strategy pursuit and differentiation strategy pursuit influence big data adoption intention through supply chain competence. This finding is consistent with the results of some previous studies that compare the associations of the two types of business strategy with functional level efficiency, and the mediating role of functional level efficiency in strategic links (Amoako-Gyampah & Acquaah, 2008; Banker, Mashruwala, & Tripathy, 2014; Ward & Duray, 2000). A managerial interpretation is that a firm's business strategy pursuit leads its functional level operations with an extensive efficiency objective, clear motivation, and planned strategic goal (Y. H. Kim, Sting, & Loch, 2014; Varadarajan, Jayachandran, & White, 2001). This goal could be cost structure oriented or differentiation oriented, or a combination of both (Hill, 1988; C. B. Li & Li, 2008; Murray, 1988). To this goal, functional level operations pursue required efficiency through acquiring and applying decision-support tools, such as big data analytics. Therefore, although there is no significant direct association between business strategy pursuit and big data analytics adoption intention, the analysis of the possible mediating effect shows that the pursuit of business strategy has an indirect effect on big data adoption intention, through its direct impact on supply chain competence which, in turn, could lead to higher big data analytics adoption intention.

Furthermore, while both cost leadership strategy and differentiation strategy are related to supply chain competence and big data analytics adoption intention, our results showed that differentiation strategy pursuit is more strongly related to supply chain competence and big data adoption intention than is cost leadership strategy pursuit, as hypothesized in H1c and H2c. This demonstrates that the complexity of a multi-faceted differentiation strategy is more difficult for firms to pursue than the efficiency-based cost leadership strategy, and thus required higher support of functional operations and business analytics capabilities. Therefore, a differentiation strategy can offer multiple and complex dimensions such as innovation and customization through which a firm can create competitive advantage, and is more difficult for competitors to imitate than a cost leadership strategy.

Finally, the post hoc analysis results revealed that when firms that are both differentiators and cost leaders are considered ambidexters, they compose a large proportion of the sample (35.3%) and, on average, tend to have higher ratings in supply chain competence and big data analytics adoption intention than firms that implement any other strategy in the typology. An explanation for this result is that ambidextrous firms tend to be more salient in strategy management and have more prominent business intent than the others, and thus are able to conduct higher pursuit for supply chain competence and higher investment for technologies. On the other hand, firms with low intent in both differentiation and cost leadership (28.4% of the sample) tend to be strategically irresolute and stuck-in-the-middle, and without a clear motivation for pursuing operational efficiency or investment for technologies. Moreover, comparing the percentage of ambidexters (35.3% of the sample) with that of the firms with a dominant business strategy, differentiators (13.4% of the sample) and cost leaders (22.9% of the sample), we see that ambidexterity is actually a relatively common practice among enterprises. Thus our findings support the literature that pure strategies may only be theoretical in principle, and a combination of business strategies is what is practiced by firms in reality (D. Miller, 1992; Parnell, 2000; Pertusa-Ortega, Molina-Azorin, & Claver-Cortes, 2009). However, while a hybrid strategy may achieve competitive advantage, it requires agile deployment and coordination of various firm resources to avoid or resolve possible conflict of interests between the two strategies, and will increase the complexity of supply chain operations, thus demand the support of more advanced business analytics capability, which motivate the management decision of big data analytics adoption. The results of our study provide empirical support for this implication.

5.2 Study Limitations and Further Research

This study reported meaningful implications regarding the development of multidimensional measures of factors that influence big data analytics adoption. However, it should be realized that the validity of an instrument cannot be firmly established on the basis of a single study. In our study, empirical data used for tests were collected from large firms based in Taiwan with operations in China. Enterprises in Taiwan are relatively efficient in supply chain operations and competitive in adopting new technologies. Furthermore, manufacturing and retail industries are the fast growing industries in Taiwan. Therefore, practitioners and researchers are suggested to interpret our findings as a reference model and be cautious when generalizing our measures to other emerging technologies or industry circumstances.

Further research efforts which focus on collecting more empirical evidences for assessing and validating firm data are recommended to overcome the limitations of the present study. Such research is suggested to address how other emerging technologies relate to business strategies and functional operations. For example, emerging technologies such as internet of things (IoT) and augmented reality (AR) have received inadequate attention from strategic considerations and technology adoption theories. Further research could also investigate the relative importance of the factors affecting each stage of the strategy shaping process. These efforts should involve studies identifying the organizational capabilities which affect business operations, information processing, and decision support. In addition, special attention could be focused on data collected in various sub-industries or specific contexts over an extended period of time. The analysis of such data may enable conclusions to be drawn about more generalized relationships among business level strategies, functional level strategies, and innovative technology adoption intention.

References

Agrawal, D., Das, S., & Abbadi, A. E. (2011). *Big data and cloud computing: Current state and future opportunities*. Paper presented at the ACM EDBT, Uppsala, Sweden.

Ajzen, I. (1991). The theory of planned behavior. *Organizational Behavior and Human Decision Processes, 50*(2), 179-211. doi:https://doi.org/10.1016/0749-5978(91)90020-T

Akter, S., Wamba, S. F., Gunasekaran, A., Dubey, R., & Childe, S. J. (2016). How to improve firm performance using big data analytics capability and business strategy alignment? *International Journal of Production Economics, 182*, 113-131. doi:10.1016/j.ijpe.2016.08.018

Amoako-Gyampah, K., & Acquaah, M. (2008). Manufacturing strategy, competitive strategy and firm performance: An empirical study in a developing economy environment. *International*

Journal of Production Economics, 111(2), 575-592. doi:10.1016/j.ijpe.2007.02.030

Angeles, R. (2005). Rfid Technologies: Supply-Chain Applications and Implementation Issues. *Information Systems Management, 22*(1), 51-65. doi:10.1201/1078/44912.22.1.20051201/85739.7

Atzori, L., Iera, A., & Morabito, G. (2010). The Internet of Things: A survey. *Computer Networks, 54*(15), 2787-2805. doi:10.1016/j.comnet.2010.05.010

Babiceanu, R. F., & Seker, R. (2016). Big Data and virtualization for manufacturing cyber-physical systems: A survey of the current status and future outlook. *Computers in Industry, 81*, 128-137. doi:10.1016/j.compind.2016.02.004

Banker, R. D., Mashruwala, R., & Tripathy, A. (2014). Does a differentiation strategy lead to more sustainable financial performance than a cost leadership strategy? *Management Decision, 52*(5), 872-896. doi:10.1108/md-05-2013-0282

Baron, R. M., & Kenny, D. A. (1986). The moderator–mediator variable distinction in social psychological research: Conceptual, strategic, and statistical considerations. *Journal of Personality and Social Psychology, 51*(6), 1173-1182. doi:10.1037/0022-3514.51.6.1173

Beamon, B. M. (1999). Measuring supply chain performance. *International Journal of Operations & Production Management, 19*(3), 275-292. doi:10.1108/01443579910249714

Borkar, V., Carey, M., & Li, C. (2012). *Inside "big data management": Ogres, onions, or parfaits?* Paper presented at the ACM EDBT/ICDT Joint Conference, Berlin, Germany.

Bryant, R. E., Katz, R. H., & Lazowska, E. D. (2008). *Big-data computing: Creating revolutionary breakthroughs in commerce, science, and society.* Paper presented at the Computing Research Initiatives for the 21st Century.

Cegielski, C. G., Allison Jones-Farmer, L., Wu, Y., & Hazen, B. T. (2012). Adoption of cloud computing technologies in supply chains: An organizational information processing theory approach. *The International Journal of Logistics Management, 23*(2), 184-211. doi:10.1108/09574091211265350

Chen, H., Chiang, R. H. L., & Storey, V. C. (2012). Business Intelligence and Analytics: From Big Data to Big Impact. *MIS Quarterly, 36*(4), 1165-1188.

Cheung, M.-S., Myers, M. B., & Mentzer, J. T. (2010). Does relationship learning lead to relationship value? A cross-national supply chain investigation. *Journal of Operations Management, 28*(6), 472-487. doi:10.1016/j.jom.2010.01.003

Cicchetti, D. V., Koenig, K., Klin, A., Volkmar, F. R., Paul, R., & Sparrow, S. (2011). From Bayes through marginal utility to effect sizes: a guide to understanding the clinical and statistical significance of the results of autism research findings. *J Autism Dev Disord, 41*(2), 168-174. doi:10.1007/s10803-010-1035-6

Claver-Cortés, E., Pertusa-Ortega, E. M., & Molina-Azorín, J. F. (2012). Characteristics of organizational structure relating to hybrid competitive strategy: Implications for performance. *Journal of Business Research, 65*(7), 993-1002. doi:10.1016/j.jbusres.2011.04.012

Cook, L. S., Heiser, D. R., & Sengupta, K. (2011). The moderating effect of supply chain role on the relationship between supply chain practices and performance. *International Journal of Physical Distribution & Logistics Management, 41*(2), 104-134. doi:10.1108/09600031111118521

Cronbach, L. (1951). Coefficient alpha and the internal structure of tests. *Psychometrika, 16*(3), 297-334. doi:10.1007/BF02310555

Davis, F. D. (1989). Perceived usefulness, perceived ease of use, and user acceptance of information technology. *MIS Quarterly, 13*(3), 319-340. Retrieved from http://search.ebscohost.com/login.aspx?direct=true&db=bth&AN=4679168&lang=zh-tw&site=ehost-live

DeGroote, S. E., & Marx, T. G. (2013). The impact of IT on supply chain agility and firm performance: An empirical investigation. *International Journal of Information Management, 33*(6), 909-916. doi:10.1016/j.ijinfomgt.2013.09.001

Dess, G. G., & Davis, P. S. (1984). Porter's (1980) Generic Strategies as Determinants of Strategic Group Membership and Organizational Performance. *Academy of Management Journal, 27*(3), 467-488. doi:10.2307/256040

Dong, S., Xu, S. X., & Zhu, K. X. (2009). Research Note—Information Technology in Supply Chains: The Value of IT-Enabled Resources Under Competition. *Information Systems Research, 20*(1),

18-32. doi:10.1287/isre.1080.0195

Fosso Wamba, S., Akter, S., Edwards, A., Chopin, G., & Gnanzou, D. (2015). How 'big data' can make big impact: Findings from a systematic review and a longitudinal case study. *International Journal of Production Economics*. doi:10.1016/j.ijpe.2014.12.031

Galbraith, J. R. (1974). Organization design: an information processing view. *Interfaces, 4*(3), 28-36. Retrieved from http://search.ebscohost.com/login.aspx?direct=true&db=bth&AN=6693280&lang=zh-tw&site=ehost-live

Glushkova, D., Jovanovic, P., & Abelló, A. (2017). Mapreduce performance model for Hadoop 2.x. *Information Systems*. doi:10.1016/j.is.2017.11.006

Gunasekaran, A., Patel, C., & McGaughey, R. E. (2004). A framework for supply chain performance measurement. *International Journal of Production*

Economics, 87(3), 333-347. doi:10.1016/j.ijpe.2003.08.003

Gunasekaran, A., Patel, C., & Tirtiroglu, E. (2001). Performance measures and metrics in a supply chain environment. *International Journal of Operations & Production Management, 21*(1/2), 71-87. doi:10.1108/01443570110358468

Hashem, I. A. T., Yaqoob, I., Anuar, N. B., Mokhtar, S., Gani, A., & Ullah Khan, S. (2015). The rise of "big data" on cloud computing: Review and open research issues. *Information Systems, 47*, 98-115. doi:10.1016/j.is.2014.07.006

Hazen, B. T., Boone, C. A., Ezell, J. D., & Jones-Farmer, L. A. (2014). Data quality for data science, predictive analytics, and big data in supply chain management: An introduction to the problem and suggestions for research and applications. *International Journal of Production Economics, 154*, 72-80. doi:10.1016/j.ijpe.2014.04.018

Hill, C. V. L. (1988). Difierentiation versus low cost or differentiation and low cost: A contingency framework. *Academy of Management Review, 13*(3), 401-412.

Huan, S. H., Sheoran, S. K., & Wang, G. (2004). A review and analysis of supply chain operations reference (SCOR) model. *Supply Chain Management: An International Journal, 9*(1), 23-29. doi:10.1108/13598540410517557

Huo, B., Qi, Y., Wang, Z., & Zhao, X. (2014). The impact of supply chain integration on firm performance. *Supply Chain Management: An International Journal, 19*(4), 369-384. doi:10.1108/scm-03-2013-0096

Janssen, M., van der Voort, H., & Wahyudi, A. (2017). Factors influencing big data decision-making quality. *Journal of Business Research, 70*, 338-345. doi:10.1016/j.jbusres.2016.08.007

Jarvis, C. B., MacKenzie, S. B., & Podsakoff, P. M.

(2003). A critical review of construct indicators and measurement model misspecification in marketing and consumer research. *Journal of consumer research, 30*(2), 199-218.

Kim, G., & Huh, M.-G. (2015). Exploration and organizational longevity: The moderating role of strategy and environment. *Asia Pacific Journal of Management, 32*(2), 389-414. doi:10.1007/s10490-014-9399-3

Kim, Y. H., Sting, F. J., & Loch, C. H. (2014). Top-down, bottom-up, or both? Toward an integrative perspective on operations strategy formation. *Journal of Operations Management, 32*(7), 462-474. doi:https://doi.org/10.1016/j.jom.2014.09.005

Koo, C. M., Koh, C. E., & Nam, K. (2004). An Examination of Porter's Competitive Strategies in Electronic Virtual Markets: A Comparison of Two On-line Business Models. *International Journal of Electronic Commerce, 9*(1), 163-180.

Kotha, S., & Vadlamani, B. L. (1995). Assessing Generic Strategies: An Empirical Investigation of Two Competing Typologies in Discrete Manufacturing Industries. *Strategic Management Journal, 16*(1), 75-83. Retrieved from http://www.jstor.org/stable/2486947

Kozlenkova, I. V., Hult, G. T. M., Lund, D. J., Mena, J. A., & Kekec, P. (2015). The Role of Marketing Channels in Supply Chain Management. *Journal of Retailing, 91*(4), 586-609. doi:10.1016/j.jretai.2015.03.003

Leidner, D. E., Lo, J., & Preston, D. (2011). An empirical investigation of the relationship of IS strategy with firm performance. *The Journal of Strategic Information Systems, 20*(4), 419-437. doi:10.1016/j.jsis.2011.09.001

Li, C. B., & Li, J. J. L. (2008). Achieving superior financial performance in China: Differentiation, cost Leadership, or both? *Journal of International*

Marketing, 16(3), 1-22.

Li, S., Ragu-Nathan, B., Ragu-Nathan, T. S., & Subba Rao, S. (2006). The impact of supply chain management practices on competitive advantage and organizational performance. *Omega, 34*(2), 107-124. doi:10.1016/j.omega.2004.08.002

Liu, H., Ke, W., Wei, K. K., Gu, J., & Chen, H. (2010). The role of institutional pressures and organizational culture in the firm's intention to adopt internet-enabled supply chain management systems. *Journal of Operations Management, 28*(5), 372-384. doi:10.1016/j.jom.2009.11.010

Lockamy, A., & McCormack, K. (2004). Linking SCOR planning practices to supply chain performance. *International Journal of Operations & Production Management, 24*(12), 1192-1218. doi:10.1108/01443570410569010

March, J. G. (1991). Exploration and Exploitation in Organizational Learning. *Organization Science,*

2(1), 71-87. Retrieved from http://www.jstor.org/stable/2634940

Mathews, J. (2016). An information processing view of competition analysis. *IUP Journal of Business Strategy, 13*(1), 7-25.

McAfee, A., & Brynjolfsson, E. (2012). Big data - The management revolution. *Harvard Business Review, October*, 1-9.

Miller, A., & Dess, G. G. (1993). Assessing Porter's (1980) model in terms of generalizability, ccuracy, and simplicity. *Journal of Management Studies, 30*(4), 553-585.

Miller, D. (1988). Relating porter's business strategies to environment and structure: analysis and performance implications. *Academy of Management Journal, 31*(2), 280-308.

Miller, D. (1992). The Generic Strategy Trap. *Journal of Business Strategy, 13*(1), 37-41. doi:10.1108/eb039467

Mintzberg, H. (1985). Strategy formation in an adhocracy. *Administrative Science Quarterly 30*(2), 160-197.

Mintzberg, H., & Waters, J. A. (1985). Of strategies, deliberate and emergent. *Strategic Management Journal, 6*(3), 257-272.

Murray, A. I. (1988). A contingency view of Porter's "generic strategies". *Academy of Management Review, 13*(3), 390-400.

Nandakumar, M. K., Ghobadian, A., & O'Regan, N. (2011). Generic strategies and performance - evidence from manufacturing firms. *International Journal of Productivity and Performance Management, 60*(3), 222-251. doi:http://dx.doi.org/10.1108/17410401111111970

Nunnally, J. C., & Bernstein, I. H. (1994). *Psychometric theory* (3 ed.). New York: McGraw-Hill.

Pagell, M., & Krause, D. R. (2002). Strategic consensus in the internal supply chain: exploring the manufacturing–purchasing link. *International Journal of Production Research, 40*(13), 3075-3092. doi:10.1080/00207540210136540

Parnell, J. A. (2000). Reframing the combination strategy debate: Defining forms of combination. *Journal of Applied Management Studies, 9*(1), 33-54. Retrieved from https://search.proquest.com/docview/213709637?accountid=10067

http://pqdd.sinica.edu.tw/twdaoapp/servlet/advanced?query=

http://sfx.lib.nccu.edu.tw/sfxlcl41?url_ver=Z39.88-2004&rft_val_fmt=info:ofi/fmt:kev:mtx:journal&genre=article&sid=ProQ:ProQ%3Aabiglobal&atitle=Reframing+the+combination+strategy+debate%3A+Defining+forms+of+combination&title=Journal+of+Applied+Management+Studies&issn=13600796&date=2000-06-01&volume=9&issue=1&spage=33&au=Parnell%2

C+John+A&isbn=&jtitle=Journal+of+Applied+Management+Studies&btitle=&rft_id=info:eric/&rft_id=info:doi/

Pertusa-Ortega, E. M., Molina-Azorin, J. F., & Claver-Cortes, E. (2009). Competitive strategies and firm Performance: A comparative analysis of pure, hybrid and stuck-in-the-middle strategies in Spanish firms. *British Journal of Management, 20*(4), 508-523. doi:10.1111/j.1467-8551.2008.00597.x

Porter, M. E. (1980). *Competitive strategy*. New York: Free Press.

Porter, M. E. (1985). *Competitive advantage*. New York: Free Press.

Porter, M. E., & Millar, V. E. (1985). How information gives you competitive advantage. *Harvard Business Review, 63*(4), 61-78.

Qi, J., Zhang, Z., Jeon, S., & Zhou, Y. (2016). Mining customer requirements from online reviews: A product improvement perspective. *Information &*

Management, 53(8), 951-963. doi:10.1016/j.im.2016.06.002

Qrunfleh, S., & Tarafdar, M. (2014). Supply chain information systems strategy: Impacts on supply chain performance and firm performance. *International Journal of Production Economics, 147*, 340-350. doi:10.1016/j.ijpe.2012.09.018

Robak, S., Franczyk, B., & Robak, M. (2013). *Applying big data and linked data concepts in supply chains management.* Paper presented at the Proceedings of the 2013 Federated Conference on Computer Science and Information Systems, Krakow, Porland.

Robinson, R. B., & Pearce, J. A. (1988). Planned Patterns of Strategic Behavior and Their Relationship to Business- Unit Performance. *Strategic Management Journal, 9*(1), 43-60. Retrieved from http://www.jstor.org/stable/2486001

Schoenherr, T., & Speier-Pero, C. (2015). Data science, predictive analytics, and big data in supply chain management: Current state and future potential. *Journal of Business Logistics, 36*(1), 120-132. doi:10.1111/jbl.12082

Shafer, J., Rixner, S., & Cox, A. L. (2010). *The hadoop distributed filesystem: Balancing portability and performance.* Paper presented at the Performance Analysis of Systems & Software (ISPASS), 2010 IEEE International Symposium on.

Smith, H. A., McKeen, J. D., & Singh, S. (2007). Developing information technology strategy for business value. *Journal of Information Technology Management, 18*(1), 49-58.

Stonebraker, M. (2010). SQL databases vs NoSQL databases. *Communications of the ACM, 53*(4), 10-11. doi:10.1145/1721654.1721659

Straub, D. W. (1989). Validating instruments in MIS research. *MIS Quarterly, 13*(2), 147-169.

Teo, H. H., Wei, K. K., & Benbasat, I. (2003). Predicting intention to adopt interganizaitonal linkages: an institutional perspective *MIS Quarterly, 27*(1), 19-49. Retrieved from http://search.ebscohost.com/login.aspx?direct=true&db=asr&AN=9284285&lang=zh-tw&site=ehost-live

Tushman, M. L., & Nadler, D. A. (1978). Information processing as an integrating concept in organizational design. *Academy of Management Review, 3*(3), 613-624.

Varadarajan, P. R., Jayachandran, S., & White, J. C. (2001). Strategic interdependence in organizations: Deconglomeration and marketing strategy. *Journal of Marketing, 65*(1), 15-28.

Venkatesh, V., & Bala, H. (2008). Technology Acceptance Model 3 and a Research Agenda on Interventions. *Decision Sciences, 39*(2), 273-315. doi:10.1111/j.1540-5915.2008.00192.x

Vijayasarathy, L. R. (2010). An investigation of moderators of the link between technology use in the supply chain and supply chain performance. *Information & Management, 47*(7-8), 364-371. doi:10.1016/j.im.2010.08.004

Wagner, S. M., Grosse-Ruyken, P. T., & Erhun, F. (2012). The link between supply chain fit and financial performance of the firm. *Journal of Operations Management, 30*(4), 340-353. doi:10.1016/j.jom.2012.01.001

Waller, M. A., & Fawcett, S. E. (2013). Data science, predictive analytics, and big data: A revolution that will transform supply chain design and management. *Journal of Business Logistics, 34*(2), 77-84.

Ward, P. T., & Duray, R. (2000). Manufacturing strategy in context environment competitive strategy and manufacturing strategy. *Journal of Operations Management, 18*, 123-138.

Weng, W. H., & Lin, W. T. (2013). A Big Data technology foresight study with scenario planning approach. *International Journal of Innovation in Management,*

1(2), 41-52.

Weng, W. H., & Lin, W. T. (2014). Development trends and strategy planning in big data industry. *Contemporary Management Research, 10*(3).

Weng, W. H., & Weng, W. T. (2013). *Forecast of development trends in big data industry*. Paper presented at the Proceedings of the Institute of Industrial Engineers Asian Conference 2013, Taipei, Taiwan.

White, A., Daniel, E. M., & Mohdzain, M. (2005). The role of emergent information technologies and systems in enabling supply chain agility. *International Journal of Information Management, 25*(5), 396-410. doi:10.1016/j.ijinfomgt.2005.06.009

Wien, A. H., & Olsen, S. O. (2017). Producing word of mouth – a matter of self-confidence? Investigating a dual effect of consumer self-confidence on WOM. *Australasian Marketing Journal (AMJ), 25*(1), 38-

45. doi:10.1016/j.ausmj.2017.01.005

Williams, F. P., D'Souza, D. E., Rosenfeldt, M. E., & Kassaee, M. (1995). Manufacturing strategy, business strategy and firm performance in a mature industry. *Journal of Operations Management, 13*(1), 19-33. doi:https://doi.org/10.1016/0272-6963(95)00006-E

Wright, P. (1987). A Refinement of Porter's generic strategies. *Strategic Management Journal, 8*, 93-101.

Wu, F., Yeniyurt, S., Kim, D., & Cavusgil, S. T. (2006). The impact of information technology on supply chain capabilities and firm performance: A resource-based view. *Industrial Marketing Management, 35*(4), 493-504. doi:10.1016/j.indmarman.2005.05.003

Wu, I.-L., & Chuang, C.-H. (2010). Examining the diffusion of electronic supply chain management with external antecedents and firm performance: A multi-stage analysis. *Decision Support Systems,*

50(1), 103-115. doi:10.1016/j.dss.2010.07.006

Xie, K., Wu, Y., Xiao, J., & Hu, Q. (2016). Value co-creation between firms and customers: The role of big data-based cooperative assets. *Information & Management,* 53(8), 1034-1048. doi:10.1016/j.im.2016.06.003